the essential barbecue cookbook

from the Home Library Test Kitchen

Cole's Home Library Cookbooks
Glen Ellen, California

the essential barbecue cookbook

Contents

Mustard honey glazed vegetables, page 92

4
Grist for the grill

The answers to all your questions about gas and charcoal cooking, plus tips on how to look after your barbecue.

8
Beef and Veal

If you still haven't ventured past steaks, check out these marvellously flavored dishes using some of the other cuts.

30
Poultry

From roast turkey to glazed duck – all done to perfection with an array of delicious sauces and accompaniments.

46
Lamb

Tandoori lamb, lamb with pistachio harissa – world-class recipes that brilliantly complement the barbecue's magic.

62
Seafood

How to grill seafood brochettes, sear a swordfish, or smoke a salmon and much, much, more.

Ginger tuna with wasabi drizzle, page 72

Sugar and rosemary smoked rump, page 29

The Essential Barbecue Cookbook...

No longer just a backyard accessory, the barbecue has moved into the mainstream of cookery. As you'll see in these pages, today's new-wave charcoal and gas-fired barbecues perform cooking techniques that will astonish you. With the recipes in this book for baking, smoking and roasting, no matter what the heat source, you're sure to be "cooking with gas"!

80
Pork
Succulent ribs, ravishing roasts, chops to die for – pork picks up flavor and favor on the barbecue.

88
Vegetables
Add these dishes to your repertoire and watch vegetables rocket up the popularity poll.

96
Breads and Desserts
If you've never tried barbecued "baked" items and desserts, you're in for a delightful surprise.

Menu Suggestions 108

Glossary 112

Index 116

Caramelized peaches with spiced yogurt, page 104

For more Cole's Home Library information on barbecuing, including cookbooks for the home barbecue chef, see page 120 or come to Cole's web site, www.coleshomelibrary.com, for an interactive tour of what is happening in the world of cooking, gardening, and crafts for today's creative lifestyle.

Grist for the grill

Gone are the days when you simply placed a sheet of metal over a couple of bricks. Nowadays, you can purchase a grill to suit every situation, ranging from very basic models right through to top-of-the-range versions featuring everything that opens and shuts. If you haven't already bought one, take the time to shop around and match your needs with the features available. Before you shop, you may wish to decide on what type of grill you're after – gas or charcoal.

Gas grills are instant, clean and easy to control. They are the most popular, as well as the more expensive. Most units have at least two burners, making it possible to cook meat over high direct heat while simultaneously cooking vegetables over low direct heat. Some have a fitted hood, offering the option of cooking with indirect heat.

Charcoal/briquette/wood grills suit people who enjoy the flavor and experience of cooking over charred wood.

a. wood b. briquettes
c. wood d. charcoal

Although they are cheaper to buy than gas and electric grills, they take longer to reach cooking heat and are messy to clean.

Getting to know your gas grill

Gas grills use one of two types of heat conductor, lava rocks or ceramic rocks, arranged over a mesh framework fitted above the burners.

Lava rocks are porous, medium to large chunks of volcanic rock that absorb heat and add flavor. The rocks can be removed and washed, then dried in sunlight before replacing them in the grill.

Ceramic rocks (sometimes called compressed lava rocks) are non-porous, disc or pyramid shapes made from a compound that includes lava rock in its makeup; they hold heat well. Ceramic rocks can be cleaned by turning them cooking-side-down and allowing the gas burners to burn off any residue that collects.

Flame-tamer grids, also known as flavor bars, are designed to reduce flare-ups; they also add an open-fire cooked flavor to food. They are available either as a cast-iron grid or a grid of vitreous enamel-coated movable bars. The vitreous enamel flame-tamer grid takes longer to heat than the cast-iron flame-tamer grid, so preheating times need to be extended if using the former.

Most gas grills are fitted with a slide-out draining tray that holds fat soak or fat absorber. The base of the tray should be lined with foil then sprinkled evenly with fat soak or absorber. Check the tray regularly and replace the fat absorber when necessary, as

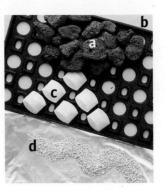

a. lava rocks b. flame-tamer grid
c. ceramic rocks d. fat soaker

accumulated fat can cause flare-ups. Most grills have a grease receptacle that must be emptied regularly to avoid flare-ups.

Getting to know your charcoal/briquette/wood grill

Charcoal, as a heat conductor, is available in hardwood or lumpwood form. Natural charcoal, most commonly made from mesquite or other kinds of hardwood, starts more quickly, burns with about twice the heat of briquettes, and smells cleaner.

Briquettes are manufactured from ground charcoal with the addition of a little coal dust and starch to help bind the mixture. They burn for a reasonable length of time and distribute the heat evenly. They may be sprinkled with spices and other seasonings to give foods a smoked flavor.

Wood is unpredictable as a heat conductor and difficult to control. It must be lit long before required for cooking to produce the bed of glowing embers that retain enough heat to complete cooking (adding more wood produces flames and smoke, which gives food an unpleasant taste). Treated wood should never be used as a fuel when grilling any food.

Cooking tips for charcoal/briquette/ wood grills

The fire is ready when the coals are covered in a layer of white ash. You should be able to hold your hand about 6 inches from the cooking rack for three to four seconds; if you cannot, the fire is too hot. If you can and don't feel any heat after a few seconds, the source has either gone out or it has not yet reached the correct cooking temperature.

Charcoal heat can, to some degree, be controlled manually. To make the fire burn hotter: shake the grill or tap the coals with metal tongs in order to remove accumulated ash. Using metal tongs, push the coals closer together; open all vents; add new/more charcoal. To make the fire burn more slowly: partially close the vents; using metal tongs, push the coals farther apart.

How much charcoal do I use?

For cooking over direct heat, one layer of charcoal should cover an area slightly larger than the food. For indirect heat, use twice the depth of coals, as they will need to burn for a longer time.

Cooking methods

There are two main methods you can use when cooking on a grill:

DIRECT HEAT also called direct cooking, direct method or open grill. This is the traditional method, where the food is placed on the grill or plate and cooked directly over the heat source. This is the best method for sausages, steaks, burgers, vegetables, and so on. A rotisserie may be used with the direct method over low burners (gas) or with an enamel baking dish below the food (charcoal) to minimize flare-ups. Food can also be wrapped in foil to protect it when using the direct method.

INDIRECT HEAT also called covered cooking or kettle cooking. With gas, the food is placed in a preheated, covered grill with the burners directly under the food turned off while the side burners remain on. With charcoal, charcoal rails (metal bars) hold two stacks of coals against the grill's sides, leaving the center of the grill rack empty. A disposable aluminum drip tray can be placed here, if desired. The food is cooked by the circulating hot air as well as by the heat conductors. This method of cooking is good for large pieces of food because it ensures that the food cooks all the way through without drying out. It is also suitable for smoking and slow-cooking.

You can also use a combination of both methods. Thick steaks or pieces of chicken, for instance, can be seared first using direct heat, then covered and cooked using indirect heat for more even cooking and juice retention.

Smoking

Smoking is a cooking style in which the flavors of the food are affected by the choice of wood used. Hickory and mesquite are the best known woods for smoking; however, there are many different varieties available, such as applewood, maple, cherry, peach or grapevine.

Wood chips have to be soaked first in cold water so that they will smolder slowly over the fire, rather than burning. For additional

flavors and scents, soak a variety of herbs and spices in the water along with your choice of wood chips.

Smoking is best suited to moderate-to-slow cooking. Instead of placing the soaked wood chips or chunks and the herbs directly onto the open flame where they burn too rapidly, put them in

a smoke box to combust slowly without causing flare-ups or unnecessary ash. During preheating, place the filled cast-iron smoke box over the heat source. When smoke appears from within the box, adjust the burners on a gas grill to low. If using a charcoal grill, place the smoke box directly under the

food and use indirect heat.

For the best results when smoking, try not to interrupt cooking with frequent opening or removal of the lid. For this reason, bear in mind that basting too frequently will lessen the intensity of the smoky flavor you want to achieve.

Grist for the grill

Preparation

To correctly "cure" or "season" the cast-iron cooking surface of a gas grill, the following steps should be followed. Most of these rules also apply to a cast-iron plate in a charcoal grill:

■ Use a light vegetable oil, such as canola, sunflower or safflower oil, and brush or lightly spray all cast-iron surfaces all over (this includes grills, plates, burners and cast-iron rock tray, if you have one).

■ Place cast-iron grill or plate in position, open hood and ignite all burners.

■ Heat grill on high, uncovered, until grill or plate begins to smoke.

■ Turn the burners down to low. Fill a bucket with cold water (no detergent); using a stiff wire brush, reserved for the purpose, scrub the grill and plate until clean.

■ Turn burners off. Lightly spray or brush grill and plate with a light vegetable oil. Your grill is now ready for you to use.

Caring for your grill

Once you have finished cooking on a gas grill, never leave it un-cleaned. The acidity from the meat fat will, with time, corrode the grill and plate.

Turn all burners to high (if you have a hood, it should remain open during cleaning). When grill or plate begins to smoke, turn gas off at the bottle (to prevent gas build-up in the hose), then at the controls. Using a stiff wire brush and cold water (no detergent), scrub the grill and plate.

Lightly spray or brush the grill or plate with a light vegetable oil before putting it away, to prevent rusting.

Invest in a vinyl cover to keep your grill looking in peak condition.

Dos & don'ts

■ Keep the grill or plate lightly oiled to prevent food from sticking.

■ Soak bamboo skewers in water to prevent them from scorching during cooking. If using metal skewers, oil them to prevent food from sticking to them.

■ Bring food to room temperature before you start cooking.

■ Trim away excess fat from meat to avoid any flare-ups during cooking.

■ Don't salt meat before cooking, as it draws out the juices. If salt is necessary, add it just before the end of cooking time.

■ Never use an aerosol cooking oil on a grill that is lighted.

corn husks

aluminum foil

banana leaves

■ When using aluminum foil, always wrap the food with the shiny side towards the food. Banana leaves and corn husks make good wrappers, too.

■ Always use glass or ceramic dishes for marinating food; metal can taint flavors.

■ To avoid burning sugar- or honey-based marinated food, cook over medium rather than high heat.

■ It is best to sear meat on each side over high heat for a few minutes, then move it to a cooler part of the grill to continue cooking as desired. Turn meat once only to retain juices and flavor, and to avoid toughening.

■ Use tongs or a slide to turn meat, (a fork pierces the meat causing loss of juices). Never cut meat to see if it is cooked; instead, press the meat with tongs – rare feels soft to touch; medium will offer a little resistance; well-done will be firm when pressed.

■ Use a meat thermometer to determine cooking time for larger cuts of meat, but NEVER leave the thermometer in the meat while it's cooking. Insert it towards the end of the cooking time and leave in for a few minutes or until the temperature stabilizes.

■ For extra-moist fish, cook whole fish unscaled; then, once cooked, peel off the skin and scales. Alternatively, cook scaled fish wrapped in foil.

■ Some sausages and spareribs are best if par-boiled before cooking to prevent excessive fat content causing flare-ups over direct heat. There is no need for par-boiling if cooking using indirect heat. Soaking sausages in an acidic marinade can also help alleviate the need to par-boil or prick them.

■ Don't use charcoal grills when it's very windy – flames are hard to control.

■ Make sure the fire is completely extinguished when the grilling is over.

■ After using a grill with a gas cylinder, make sure it is turned off properly to extinguish the flame.

Accessories and additions

■ Gas fuse: essential for safety and convenience when using gas grills. An invention that prevents gas leaks and possibly disastrous gas explosions, it is placed between the cylinder bottle and the regulator or hose supply of LP gas cylinders.

■ Roast holder and rack: the upper section of all covered grills is hotter than the grill level because of rising heat and the heat absorbed by the hood. Roast holders and racks are great to use to elevate the food from the grill for even cooking and browning. With two prongs that you insert into the food, the rack is an excellent alternative to a rotisserie.

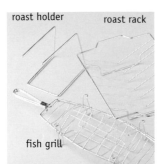

roast holder   roast rack

fish grill

■ Fish grill: also known as fish cage or basket. Available in varying sizes to hold different quantities/sizes of fish. Can be used with indirect or direct cooking.

■ Meat thermometer: takes the guesswork out of cooking time, especially for thicker cuts of meat.

■ Firestarters: also called firelighters, are helpful in getting the fire going. Solid blocks or in liquid form.

■ Side burner: great for stir-frying, heating sauces, deep-frying and so on, outdoors.

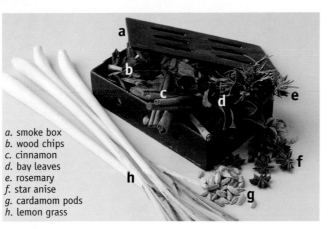

a. smoke box
b. wood chips
c. cinnamon
d. bay leaves
e. rosemary
f. star anise
g. cardamom pods
h. lemon grass

■ Smoke box: a cast-iron box that is filled with smoking chips. Air holes allow a smoky flavor to be imparted to grilled foods.

■ Smoking chips: available in many different woods; suitable for use in a smoke box or in a baking dish.

vegetable rack

■ Vegetable rack: has prongs for securing vegetables.

■ Stiff wire cleaning brush: ideal for removing charred food from grill or plate.

■ Charcoal chimney: also known as fire-lighting hood and used when lighting charcoal. It is a metal cylinder with a handle and air holes on the side.

■ Grill tool set: spatulas, long-handled tongs, basting brushes, forks, skewers and knives can all be found in grill tool sets.

■ Rotisserie: battery-operated rotisseries are available and can be used with both direct and indirect heat. When mounting food on a rotisserie, make sure it is well-centered and properly balanced – uneven weight

distribution can place strain on the motor. To avoid flare-ups, cook on rotisserie using indirect heat and place an enamel tray filled with water or wine under the food.

■ Disposable baking dish: for use with indirect heat and smoking. They are usually made of aluminum (or use an inexpensive roasting tray from the supermarket).

■ Grill plates and grills: additional plates and grills are available for gas and charcoal grills.

disposable baking dish

kebab rack

cast-iron plate

■ Kebab rack: used to elevate food and ensure even cooking and browning.

■ Warming rack: used to keep food warm with direct heat, or to cook food by the indirect heat method.

warming rack

Cook on ...

■ **Cooking times given throughout the book are to be used as a guide only.**

■ Before you use your grill for the first time, be sure to read through the manufacturer's instructions closely and thoroughly.

■ Organization is the key to successful grilling. Have all utensils, sauces and so on within arm's reach before you begin so you won't have to leave the fire untended.

■ Start with a clean grill or grill plate, i.e., one that's free of burned-on food from previous usage.

■ Thoroughly heat the grill before starting to cook. This may take only 5 to 10 minutes for gas, but up to an hour for charcoal or wood-fired grills.

■ The grill hood or lid must be in the open position when lighting the grill. If gas, once all the burners are on, close hood and preheat on high for about 5 minutes. If you have a fitted hood, but are cooking using direct heat, preheat the grill, uncovered, for about 5 to 10 minutes.

■ Cooking time is affected by factors such as atmospheric conditions, temperature of the fire and food, type of fuel used, and how much food is being cooked at the one time. Each time the hood or lid is opened, heat is released and cooking time must be increased. Therefore, cooking times may vary. To avoid over-cooking, start testing the food a little earlier than the time suggested in the recipe for doneness, say 5 or 10 minutes – no more or you will lose essential heat.

■ When cooking on a gas grill, keep a spray bottle filled with water handy to douse flare-ups. Use this method only as a last resort when cooking with wood or charcoal, because the water will cause ash to rise and settle on the food.

Beef and Veal

From ribs to roasts, rib-eye or rump, we can't think of a single cut of beef or veal that doesn't taste twice as good grilled outdoors as it does when cooked in the house. Meat and the grill are a match made in heaven... together, it seems, practically since man discovered fire. And it's little wonder – beef's full flavor, sumptuous juices and seductive aromas are all enlivened by a dash of summer and smoke.

BEEF AND HALOUMI KEBABS WITH CAPER BUTTER

Soak bamboo skewers in water for about 1 hour to prevent them from scorching.

2lb rump steak, cubed
3 tablespoons olive oil
1¹/₂ tablespoons grated lemon rind
3 tablespoons lemon juice
1¹/₂ tablespoons grated
  fresh horseradish
12oz haloumi or fontina
  cheese, cubed
8 medium corn tortillas

CAPER BUTTER
3 tablespoons drained capers, chopped
7 tablespoons butter, melted

Place beef in large shallow dish with combined oil, rind, juice and horseradish. *[Best made ahead to this stage. Cover, refrigerate 3 hours or overnight.]*
  Thread beef and cheese on 8 skewers; cook on heated oiled grill until browned all over and cooked as desired. Meanwhile, wrap tortillas in foil in packets of 4 and heat on grill. Remove tortillas from foil, wrap each skewer in a tortilla. To serve, remove skewers, if desired, leaving beef and cheese enclosed; accompany with Caper Butter.

Caper Butter Combine capers and butter in small bowl.

SERVES 4

BEEF AND VEGETABLE TEPPAN YAKI

4 filet mignon steaks
¹/₄ cup soy sauce
3 tablespoons mirin
3 tablespoons sake
1 teaspoon grated fresh ginger
2 teaspoons brown sugar
1 clove garlic, crushed
8oz snow peas
8oz asparagus

Place beef in large bowl with combined soy, mirin, sake, ginger, sugar and garlic. *[Best made ahead to this stage. Cover, refrigerate 3 hours or overnight.]*
  Steam or microwave snow peas and asparagus, separately, until just tender; drain. Drain beef over medium bowl; place vegetables in bowl with reserved marinade. Cook beef on heated oiled grill until browned on both sides and cooked as desired. Meanwhile, towards end of beef cooking time, drain vegetables; discard marinade. Cook vegetables, alongside beef on grill, until browned all over.

SERVES 4

From left Beef and vegetable teppan yaki; Beef and haloumi kebabs with caper butter

RIB STEAKS WITH BELL PEPPER PESTO AND MASHED SWEET POTATOES

4 beef rib steaks (with bone in)

BELL PEPPER PESTO
2 large sweet red bell peppers, seeded, quartered
1/2 cup sun-dried tomatoes in oil, drained
1 1/2 tablespoons grated fresh ginger
1 1/2 tablespoons olive oil
1 teaspoon sugar
3 tablespoons finely chopped fresh basil

MASHED SWEET POTATOES
2 large orange sweet potatoes, chopped
1 large potato, chopped
1/4 cup cream
1 clove garlic, crushed
1 teaspoon ground cumin

Cook beef on heated oiled grill until browned on both sides and cooked as desired. Serve steaks, topped with Bell Pepper Pesto, on Mashed Sweet Potatoes.

Bell Pepper Pesto Blend or process peppers until almost smooth; strain, discard liquid. Blend or process sun-dried tomatoes, ginger, oil and sugar. Place mixture in medium bowl; stir in pepper puree and basil.

Mashed Sweet Potatoes Boil, steam or microwave sweet potatoes and potato, separately, until tender; drain. Mash together with cream, garlic and cumin.

SERVES 4

NEW YORK CUT STEAKS IN HERBED MUSHROOM SAUCE

4 boneless sirloin steaks (New York cut)
2/3 cup dry red wine
1 1/2 tablespoons cream style horseradish
2 teaspoons finely chopped fresh lemon thyme
1 1/2 tablespoons olive oil
1 1/2 tablespoons brown sugar
2 tablespoons butter
1 large white onion, sliced
1 clove garlic, crushed
1lb button mushrooms, sliced
1/4 cup beef stock
1 1/2 tablespoons chopped fresh parsley

Place beef in large shallow dish with 1/2 cup of the wine, 2 teaspoons of the horseradish, 1 teaspoon of the thyme, and all of the oil and sugar. [Best made ahead to this stage. Cover, refrigerate

3 hours or overnight.]
  Cook beef on heated oiled grill until browned on both sides and cooked as desired. Meanwhile, melt butter in large pan on grill; cook onion and garlic, stirring, until onion is soft. Add mushrooms; cook until soft. Add remaining horseradish, thyme and wine with stock; simmer, uncovered, about 5 minutes or until most of the liquid has evaporated. Stir in parsley. Serve beef with herbed mushroom sauce.

SERVES 4

VEAL SHOULDER WITH SPICED COUSCOUS

1 cup couscous
1 cup boiling water
2 tablespoons butter
1 medium yellow onion, chopped finely
1 clove garlic, crushed
2 teaspoons ground cumin
2 teaspoons ground turmeric
1 1/2 tablespoons caraway seeds, toasted
3 tablespoons finely chopped fresh cilantro

1/3 cup lemon juice
4lb veal shoulder, boned
3 tablespoons olive oil

Combine couscous and measured amount of boiling water in medium heatproof bowl; cover, stand about 5 minutes or until water is absorbed. Using fork, toss couscous to separate grains.
  Melt butter in small pan; cook onion and garlic, stirring, until onion is soft. Combine onion mixture with couscous; add cumin, turmeric, caraway, cilantro and half the juice. Place veal, cut-side-up, on board. Place couscous mixture in center of veal; roll tightly, secure with string. [Best made just before cooking.]
  Place veal in disposable baking dish; drizzle with oil and remaining juice. Cook in covered grill, using indirect heat, following manufacturer's instructions, about 40 minutes or until browned all over and cooked as desired.

SERVES 6

Left, from top New York cut steaks in herbed mushroom sauce; Rib steaks with bell pepper pesto and mashed sweet potatoes
Above Veal shoulder with spiced couscous

BEEF FAJITAS

1lb beef tenderloin, sliced thinly
1/3 cup barbecue sauce
1 teaspoon ground cumin
1 teaspoon ground coriander
1/2 teaspoon chili powder
**1 small sweet red bell pepper,
    seeded, sliced**
**1 small sweet green bell pepper,
    seeded, sliced**
**1 small sweet yellow bell pepper,
    seeded, sliced**
8 large flour tortillas
3/4 cup sour cream

AVOCADO TOPPING
2 medium avocados
1 1/2 tablespoons lime juice
1 clove garlic, crushed

TOMATO SALSA
**2 medium tomatoes,
    seeded, chopped**
1 small red onion, chopped
1 1/2 tablespoons olive oil
**2 teaspoons chopped
    fresh cilantro**

Place beef in medium bowl with sauce, cumin, cilantro and chili. *[Best made ahead to this stage. Cover, refrigerate for 3 hours or overnight.]*

Cook bell pepper slices on heated oiled grill plate until browned; remove from heat. Cook beef on heated oiled grill until browned and cooked as desired. Return peppers to grill with beef and cook just until hot.

Meanwhile, wrap tortillas in foil in packets of 4 and heat on grill. Remove tortillas from foil and divide beef mixture among them. Top with sour cream, Avocado Topping and Tomato Salsa.

Avocado Topping Mash both avocados coarsely in a medium bowl with a fork; mash in the lime juice and garlic.

Tomato Salsa Combine all ingredients in a small bowl.

SERVES 4

INDIAN SPICED BEEF WITH DAL

3 tablespoons cumin seeds
1 1/2 tablespoons coriander seeds
2 teaspoons sweet paprika
2 teaspoons ground cinnamon
1 teaspoon ground cardamom
1 teaspoon chili powder
5 cloves garlic, crushed
2 teaspoons grated fresh ginger
1/4 cup peanut oil
4lb beef rump roast

Bowls from Olson & Blake Collectables

DAL
1 1/2 cups red lentils
1/4 cup shredded fresh mint
4 cups vegetable stock

Cook cumin and coriander seeds, paprika, cinnamon, cardamom and chili powder in dry medium pan, stirring, until fragrant. Place seed mixture in small bowl with garlic, ginger and oil; mix to a paste. Trim as much fat from beef as possible; spread paste all over beef. *[Best made ahead to this stage. Cover, refrigerate at least 3 hours or overnight.]*

Place beef on roasting rack or basket, or in disposable baking dish. Cook in covered grill, using indirect heat, following manufacturer's instructions, about 1 hour 20 minutes or until browned all over and cooked as desired. Remove from heat, cover; stand 10 minutes before slicing. Serve with Dal.

Dal Combine lentils, mint and stock in medium pan. Bring to boil; simmer, uncovered, stirring occasionally, about 15 minutes or until lentils are tender.

SERVES 8

Left Beef fajitas
Above Indian spiced beef with dal

VEAL MEDALLIONS WITH TAPENADE

2 cups firmly packed fresh parsley
1/2 cup pitted black olives
3 tablespoons drained capers
1 1/2 tablespoons lemon juice
1 clove garlic, crushed
4 veal eye medallions
8 slices paper-thin prosciutto

Blend or process parsley until finely chopped. With motor operating, add olives, capers, juice and garlic; blend until almost smooth. *[Can be made ahead to this stage. Cover, refrigerate up to 1 week.]*

Spread olive mixture around the edge of each medallion; wrap 2 slices prosciutto around each piece to cover olive mixture, secure with toothpicks. Cook veal on heated oiled grill until browned on both sides and cooked as desired. Just before serving, remove toothpicks.

SERVES 4

VEAL PARMIGIANA

2 teaspoons olive oil
1 medium white onion,
   chopped finely
2 cloves garlic, crushed
14 1/2 oz can tomatoes
1/4 cup tomato paste
1 1/2 tablespoons balsamic vinegar
1 teaspoon sugar
1 1/2 tablespoons shredded
   fresh basil
2 small eggplants
8 veal scaloppine slices
1 1/2 cups grated pizza cheese

Heat oil in small pan; cook onion and garlic, stirring, until onion is soft. Add undrained crushed tomatoes, paste, vinegar and sugar; simmer, uncovered, about 10 minutes or until sauce thickens, stir in basil. *[Can be made a day ahead to this stage. Cover, refrigerate overnight.]*

Meanwhile, cut unpeeled eggplants into 1/2 inch slices; cook on heated oiled grill until browned on both sides. Cook veal on heated oiled grill until browned on one side. Turn veal, top with sauce, eggplant and cheese; cook until cheese is melted and veal is cooked as desired.

SERVES 4 TO 6

From left Veal parmigiana; Veal medallions with tapenade

VEAL RIB CHOPS WITH A THREE-BEAN SALAD

**1 cup dried
   black-eyed peas
2 teaspoons cumin seeds
2 teaspoons ground coriander
3 tablespoons chopped
   fresh mint
1/2 cup olive oil
4 drained sun-dried tomatoes
   in oil, chopped
1 1/2 tablespoons cider vinegar
1 clove garlic, crushed
8 veal rib chops
5oz green beans
1 1/2 cups frozen fava beans,
   cooked, peeled**

Place black-eyed peas in large bowl, cover with water; cover, stand overnight.

Drain peas; place in large pan of boiling water. Simmer, uncovered, for about 30 minutes or until peas are tender; drain. *[Can be made ahead to this stage. Cover, refrigerate overnight.]*

Add spices to heated dry pan; cook, stirring, until fragrant. Blend or process spices, mint, oil, tomato, vinegar and garlic until smooth. Place chops in large bowl with half of the spice mixture. *[Can be made ahead to this stage. Cover, refrigerate overnight or freeze.]*

Cook chops on heated oiled grill until browned on both sides and cooked as desired. Meanwhile, boil, steam or microwave green beans until tender; drain. Combine all beans and peas with remaining spice mixture in bowl; serve with chops.

SERVES 4

VEAL SCALOPPINE WITH LEMON AND THYME SAUCE

**4 tablespoons butter
1 egg yolk
1 1/2 tablespoons sweet chili sauce
1 teaspoon grated lemon rind
3 tablespoons lemon juice
2 teaspoons chopped fresh thyme
8 veal scaloppine slices**

Melt butter in small pan; add egg yolk, sauce, rind and juice. Cook, stirring, over low heat, without boiling, until sauce thickens slightly. Stir in thyme; cool. Cover and refrigerate until just set. *[Can be made ahead to this stage. Cover, refrigerate overnight.]*

Spread half the sauce over both sides of veal; cook veal on heated oiled grill until browned on both sides and cooked as desired. Just before serving, spread veal with remaining sauce.

SERVES 4 TO 6

BEEF SAUSAGES WITH CARAMELIZED ONIONS

Order sausage casing from the butcher.

2lb ground beef
2 cups fresh breadcrumbs
$^1/_2$ cup dry red wine
$^1/_4$ cup tomato paste
2 teaspoons chopped fresh oregano
1 teaspoon chopped fresh thyme
1 teaspoon cracked black pepper
6 feet sausage casing

CARAMELIZED ONIONS
3 tablespoons butter
4 large yellow onions, sliced
1 clove garlic, crushed
3 tablespoons brown sugar
1$^1/_2$ tablespoons balsamic vinegar
3 tablespoons beef stock

Combine beef, breadcrumbs, wine, paste, herbs and pepper in large bowl. Place half of the beef mixture into large piping bag fitted with $^3/_4$ inch plain tube. Tie a knot at one end of sausage casing. Open other end of casing, place over tube; work all of casing onto tube.

Pipe beef mixture into casing, twisting casing at 4 inch intervals for individual sausages. Repeat with remaining beef

mixture. *[Can be made ahead to this stage. Cover, refrigerate overnight or freeze.]*

Cook sausages on heated oiled grill until browned all over and cooked through. Serve with Caramelized Onions.

Caramelized Onions Melt butter in medium pan on grill; cook onion and garlic, stirring, until onion is soft and browned. Add sugar, vinegar and stock; cook, stirring, until thick and syrupy.

MAKES ABOUT 20 SAUSAGES

Left, from top Veal rib chops with a three-bean salad; Veal scaloppine with lemon and thyme sauce
Above Beef sausages with caramelized onions

GREEK-STYLE BEEF WITH TZATZIKI AND SALAD

1/4 cup lemon juice
1/4 cup olive oil
1/3 cup chopped fresh oregano
2 cloves garlic, crushed
3 tablespoons dry white wine
4 beef T-bone steaks

TZATZIKI
3/4 cup yogurt
1 clove garlic, crushed
2 teaspoons lemon juice
1 medium cucumber,
  chopped finely
1/2 teaspoon ground cumin
11/2 tablespoons chopped
  fresh mint

GARLIC ARUGULA SALAD
11/2 tablespoons dry white wine
11/2 tablespoons lemon juice
2 teaspoons olive oil
2 cloves garlic, crushed
8oz torn arugula leaves
4oz baby spinach leaves

Combine juice, oil, oregano, garlic and wine in large bowl; add beef to marinade. *[Must be made ahead to this stage. Cover, refrigerate 3 hours or overnight.]*
Drain beef; discard marinade. Cook beef on heated oiled grill until browned on both sides and cooked as desired. Serve beef with Tzatziki and Garlic Arugula Salad.

Tzatziki Combine all ingredients in small bowl.

Garlic Arugula Salad Combine wine, juice, oil and garlic in jar; shake well. In large bowl gently toss arugula, spinach and dressing.

SERVES 4

JAZZY BEEF SAUSAGES

1/4 cup barbecue sauce
11/2 tablespoons Worcestershire
  sauce
11/2 tablespoons tomato ketchup
1 clove garlic, crushed
8 thick beef sausages
2 medium yellow
  onions, sliced

Combine sauces, ketchup and garlic in small bowl. Cook sausages and onion on heated oiled grill, brushing occasionally with sauce mixture, until browned all over and cooked through.

SERVES 4

NACHOS SAUSAGES

8 thick beef sausages
11/2 oz packet cheese corn chips,
  crushed coarsely
2/3 cup mild chunky salsa
2/3 cup pizza cheese

Cook sausages on heated oiled grill until browned all over and cooked through. Cut a slit down the length of each sausage, not cutting through.
Sprinkle sausages with corn chips, top with salsa and cheese. Return sausages to grill, cook until cheese melts.

SERVES 4

SAUSAGES WITH GARLIC MUSHROOMS

3 tablespoons butter
2 cloves garlic, crushed
5oz button mushrooms, sliced
2 teaspoons Dijon mustard
11/2 tablespoons dry white wine
8 thick beef sausages

Heat butter in medium pan, add garlic and mushrooms; cook, stirring, until mushrooms are tender and browned lightly. Add mustard and wine, cook, stirring, until nearly all the liquid has evaporated. Cook sausages on heated oiled grill until browned all over and cooked through. Serve sausages with garlic mushrooms.

SERVES 4

SAUSAGES WITH MAPLE SYRUP AND MUSTARD

11/2 tablespoons butter
1/4 cup maple syrup
11/2 tablespoons Dijon mustard
1/2 cup orange juice
12 thin beef sausages

Combine butter, syrup, mustard and juice in small pan; stir over low heat until ingredients are combined. Cook sausages on heated oiled grill, brushing occasionally with maple syrup mixture, until browned all over and cooked through.

SERVES 4

Top, from left Sausages with garlic mushrooms, Nachos sausages, Sausages with maple syrup and mustard, Jazzy beef sausages; Greek-style beef with tzatziki and salad

BEEF WITH SPICED SEA SALT CRUST

3 tablespoons dried juniper berries, chopped
3 tablespoons grated lemon rind
1¹/₂ tablespoons sea salt
1¹/₂ tablespoons cracked black pepper
2 teaspoons ground cumin
4lb beef sirloin roast

Combine berries, rind, salt, pepper and cumin in small bowl; press onto beef. *[Best made ahead to this stage. Cover, refrigerate 3 hours or overnight.]*

Place beef on roasting rack or basket, or in disposable baking dish. Cook in covered grill, using indirect heat, following manufacturer's instructions, about 1 hour 20 minutes or until browned all over and cooked as desired. Remove from heat, cover; let stand 10 minutes before slicing and serving.

SERVES 8 TO 10

BEEF WITH BRANDIED WALNUTS AND PRUNES

1¹/₃lb boneless beef rump
¹/₃ cup walnut oil
¹/₃ cup cider vinegar
¹/₃ cup brown sugar
1¹/₂ cups pitted prunes, halved
1 cup walnut pieces, chopped coarsely
¹/₃ cup brandy
5 tablespoons butter

Place beef in large bowl with combined walnut oil, vinegar and sugar. *[Best made ahead to this stage. Cover, refrigerate for 3 hours or overnight.]*

Drain beef over medium pan; reserve marinade. Cook beef on heated oiled grill until well browned all over. Place beef on roasting rack or basket, or in disposable baking dish. Cook in covered grill, using indirect heat, following manufacturer's instructions, about 40 minutes or until browned all over and cooked as desired. Remove from heat, cover; let stand 10 minutes before slicing and serving.

Meanwhile, combine reserved marinade with prunes, nuts, brandy and butter. Bring to boil; simmer, uncovered, for 5 minutes. Serve brandied walnuts and prunes with beef.

SERVES 4

Left from top Beef with spiced sea salt crust; Beef with brandied walnuts and prunes

BURGERS BELLISSIMO

1 large sweet red bell pepper
2 cloves garlic, crushed
1 small white onion, chopped
1/4 cup sun-dried tomatoes in oil,
   drained, chopped coarsely
3 tablespoons sun-dried
   tomato pesto
2lb ground beef
7oz feta cheese, crumbled
1 large red onion, sliced
2 large tomatoes,
   sliced thickly
8 bread rolls
4oz mesclun

AVOCADO DRESSING

1 medium avocado
1/3 cup buttermilk
11/2 tablespoons lemon juice

Quarter pepper, remove and discard seeds and membrane. Roast under broiler or in very hot oven, skin-side-up, until skin blisters and blackens. Cover pepper pieces in plastic or paper for 5 minutes; peel away and discard skin, chop flesh roughly. Blend or process pepper, garlic, white onion, sun-dried tomato and pesto until smooth. Combine vegetable mixture in large bowl with beef; shape mixture into 8 patties. Cover, refrigerate 30 minutes. *[Can be made ahead to this stage. Cover, refrigerate overnight or freeze.]*

Cook patties on heated oiled grill until browned on one side; turn, sprinkle with cheese, cook until patties are browned and cooked through.

Meanwhile, cook red onion and tomato slices on heated oiled grill until onion is browned lightly and tomato is browned on both sides. Split rolls; toast. Spread bases with some of the Avocado Dressing; top with mesclun, patties, onion and tomato. Drizzle burgers with remaining Dressing.

Avocado Dressing Blend or process all ingredients until smooth. *[Can be made a few hours ahead. Cover, refrigerate.]*

MAKES 8

MEGA BEEF BURGERS

2lb ground beef
1 small yellow onion,
   chopped finely
2 cloves garlic, crushed
3 tablespoons barbecue sauce
3 tablespoons Worcestershire sauce
2 teaspoons seasoned salt
3 tablespoons chopped fresh parsley
1/2 cup fresh bread crumbs
1 egg, beaten lightly
2 large yellow onions,
   extra, sliced
12 slices bacon, halved
6 eggs, extra
6 bread rolls
3oz mesclun

Combine beef in large bowl with small yellow onion, garlic, sauces, salt, parsley, breadcrumbs and egg; shape mixture into 6 patties. *[Can be made ahead to this stage. Cover, refrigerate overnight or freeze.]*

Cook patties on heated oiled grill until browned on both sides and cooked through. Meanwhile, cook extra onion, bacon and extra eggs on heated oiled grill until onion is soft, bacon crisp and eggs cooked as desired. Split rolls; toast. Sandwich mesclun, burgers, onion, bacon and eggs between roll halves.

MAKES 6

Below, from left Mega beef burgers;
Burgers bellissimo

BALSAMIC AND GINGER BEEF

1/2 cup olive oil
1/4 cup balsamic vinegar
1 1/2 tablespoons grated fresh ginger
1 teaspoon brown sugar
1 teaspoon soy sauce
4 thick T-bone steaks

Combine oil, vinegar, ginger, sugar and sauce in jar; shake well. Reserve 1/4 cup of the vinegar mixture; brush steaks all over using about half of the rest of the mixture. *[Best made ahead to this stage. Cover, refrigerate for 3 hours or overnight.]*

Cook beef on heated oiled grill until browned on both sides. Cook in covered grill, using indirect heat, following manufacturer's instructions, for about 30 minutes or until cooked as desired, brushing beef occasionally with what remains of the brushing mixture. Remove beef from heat, cover; let stand for about 10 minutes. Just before serving, pour reserved vinegar mixture over beef.

SERVES 4

SWEET CHILI BEEF RIBS

3lb beef spareribs
1/2 cup sweet chili sauce
1 1/2 tablespoons soy sauce
1/4 cup rice wine
2 cloves garlic, crushed
1 teaspoon grated fresh ginger
3 tablespoons finely chopped fresh cilantro

Place spareribs in large shallow dish with combined sauces, wine, garlic, ginger and cilantro. *[Best made ahead to this stage. Cover tightly, refrigerate 4 hours or overnight, or freeze.]*

Cook ribs in covered grill, using indirect heat, following manufacturer's instructions, about 30 minutes or until browned all over and cooked as desired.

SERVES 4

Above Balsamic and ginger beef
Right Sweet chili beef ribs

BEEF RIB ROAST WITH RED PEPPER CRUST

3lb standing rib roast
1/3 cup olive oil
1/4 cup chopped fresh lemon thyme
2 cloves garlic, crushed
**1 large sweet red bell pepper,
    seeded, chopped**
1/2 cup pine nuts, toasted
1 clove garlic, crushed, extra

Place beef in large shallow dish with combined 1/4 cup of the oil, 3 tablespoons of the thyme and 2 cloves crushed garlic. *[Best made ahead to this stage. Cover, refrigerate 3 hours or overnight.]*

Blend or process pepper until almost smooth; strain, discard liquid. Return pepper puree to blender; add pine nuts, extra garlic and remaining thyme and oil, process until smooth. *[Can be made ahead to this stage. Cover, refrigerate overnight.]*

Place beef on roasting rack or basket, or in disposable baking dish. Cook in covered grill, using indirect heat, following manufacturer's instructions, about 40 minutes. Spread beef with pepper paste; cook about 20 minutes or until cooked as desired.

SERVES 4 TO 6

STANDING RIB ROAST PROVENÇAL

3lb standing rib roast
2 cups dry red wine
3 tablespoons olive oil
3 cloves garlic, sliced
2 teaspoons chopped fresh thyme
2 teaspoons chopped fresh rosemary
**3 medium white
    onions, quartered**
4 bay leaves

Place beef in large shallow dish with combined wine, oil, garlic, herbs, onions and leaves. *[Best made ahead to this stage. Cover, refrigerate 3 hours or overnight.]*

Drain beef and onions over small pan; reserve marinade. Bring marinade to boil; simmer, uncovered, until reduced by half.

Cook beef on heated oiled grill until browned all over. Place beef and onions on roasting rack or basket, or in disposable baking dish. Cook in covered grill, using indirect heat, following manufacturer's instructions, and brushing occasionally with marinade, about 1 hour or until cooked as desired.

SERVES 4 TO 6

From left Standing rib roast provençal;
Beef rib roast with red pepper crust

China and napery from Bed, Bath 'n' Table

BRAISED VINEGARED BEEF WITH CHINESE GREENS

1³/4lb rump steak, sliced thinly
1¹/2 tablespoons lime juice
1¹/2 tablespoons grated fresh ginger
2 cloves garlic, crushed
1¹/2 tablespoons finely shredded fresh basil
1 teaspoon sugar
1¹/2 tablespoons vegetable oil
2 teaspoons dark sesame oil
1 medium white onion, sliced finely
1 small Chinese cabbage, shredded

14oz bok choy, shredded
13oz choy sum, shredded
3 tablespoons balsamic vinegar
8oz tat soi leaves
5oz snow peas
1¹/2 tablespoons sesame seeds, toasted

Combine beef in large bowl with juice, ginger, garlic, basil and sugar. *[Best made ahead to this stage. Cover, refrigerate at least 3 hours or overnight.]*

Drain beef; discard marinade. Heat half of the combined oils in wok; stir-fry onion until soft. Add beef; stir-fry, in batches, until browned and cooked as desired. Transfer beef mixture to large bowl. Add cabbage, bok choy, choy sum, half of the vinegar and remaining oils to wok; stir-fry until just wilted, add to bowl with beef. Add tat soi, snow peas and remaining vinegar to wok; stir-fry until just wilted. Return beef and vegetables to wok; gently toss over heat until heated through, sprinkle with sesame seeds.

SERVES 4 TO 6

Above, from top Stir-fried beef with blood orange; Braised vinegared beef with Chinese greens
Right Port-smoked beef

STIR-FRIED BEEF WITH BLOOD ORANGE

You need 3 blood oranges (or substitute 4 regular oranges) for this recipe.

1¼lb rump steak, sliced thinly
¼ cup light olive oil
12 star anise
3 tablespoons finely grated blood orange rind
½ cup blood orange juice
3 tablespoons peanut oil
1 medium red onion, sliced
2 cloves garlic, crushed
1½ tablespoons grated fresh ginger
4 baby bok choy, sliced
½ cup dried currants
2 blood oranges, sectioned
3 tablespoons soy sauce
3 tablespoons oyster sauce

Place beef in medium bowl with olive oil, star anise, rind and half of the juice. *[Best made ahead to this stage. Cover, refrigerate 6 hours or overnight.]*

Drain beef; discard marinade. Heat half the peanut oil in wok or large pan; stir-fry beef, in batches, until browned and almost cooked. Heat remaining oil in wok; stir-fry onion, garlic and ginger until soft. Add bok choy and currants; stir-fry until bok choy is just wilted. Return beef to wok, add orange sections remaining juice and combined sauces; stir-fry about 1 minute or until beef is hot and sauce slightly thickened.

SERVES 4

PORT-SMOKED BEEF

You need 8oz smoking chips for this recipe.

3lb beef tenderloin
3 tablespoons olive oil
2 cloves garlic, crushed
¼ cup port
3 tablespoons chopped fresh oregano
1 cup port, extra

Place beef in large bowl with combined oil, garlic, port and oregano. *[Best made ahead to this stage. Cover, refrigerate for 6 hours or overnight.]*

Combine smoking chips and extra port in small bowl; let stand 2 hours. Cook beef on heated oiled grill just until browned all over; place beef in disposable baking dish. Place drained smoking chips in smoke box; place beside beef on grill. Cook in covered grill, using indirect heat, following manufacturer's instructions, 1 hour 30 minutes or until cooked as desired.

SERVES 4 TO 6

Plates from Country Road

SUGAR AND ROSEMARY SMOKED RUMP

You need 12oz briquettes for this recipe.

25 sprigs fresh rosemary
2/3 cup white sugar
2¼lb beef rump roast

Place briquettes in large disposable baking dish; light briquettes according to manufacturer's instructions. When flame subsides and briquettes are coated with ash, sprinkle with rosemary and sugar. Place beef on wire cake rack; place rack over briquettes. Cover beef loosely with foil and cook in covered grill, using indirect heat, following manufacturer's instructions, about 40 minutes or until cooked as desired.

SERVES 4 TO 6

THAI BEEF SALAD

1lb beef rump steak
2 English cucumbers
5 large plum tomatoes
2 cups bean sprouts, trimmed
1½ tablespoons small fresh mint leaves

THAI DRESSING
¼ cup sweet chili sauce
1½ tablespoons fish sauce
1½ tablespoons lime juice
1 clove garlic, crushed
3 tablespoons chopped fresh cilantro
1½ tablespoons chopped fresh mint

Brush beef with ¼ cup of the Thai Dressing. *[Best made ahead to this stage. Cover, refrigerate 3 hours or overnight.]*

Cook beef on heated oiled grill until browned on both sides and cooked as desired. Remove from heat, cover; let stand for 10 minutes before slicing thinly. Meanwhile, halve cucumbers lengthwise, scoop out and discard seeds; slice thinly. Cut tomatoes in quarters lengthwise, remove and discard seeds; slice thinly. Just before serving, toss beef in medium bowl with cucumber, tomato, sprouts and remaining Dressing; sprinkle with small unchopped mint leaves.

Thai Dressing Combine all ingredients in jar; shake well. *[Can be made a few hours ahead. Cover tightly, refrigerate.]*

SERVES 4

Left Sugar and rosemary smoked rump
Above Thai beef salad

BEEF AND VEAL 29

Poultry

Grilling elevates this already versatile meat to the realm of the inspired. When that quality of versatility possessed naturally by chicken and other poultry comes into contact with a sizzling grill, great food happens. Poultry is ready to eat if, when pierced, its juices run clear. Because this succulent meat can quickly become overcooked, bird-watching must be a part of the grilling process.

DRUMSTICKS WITH CRUNCHY SATAY SAUCE

8 chicken drumsticks
1¹/₂ tablespoons grated fresh ginger
1 clove garlic, crushed
1 cup coconut milk
3 tablespoons lime juice
3 tablespoons soy sauce
1¹/₂ tablespoons honey
1 cup finely chopped unsalted roasted peanuts
1 teaspoon Madras curry powder
1¹/₂ tablespoons ground coriander

Make 2 deep cuts in thickest part of each drumstick. Combine remaining ingredients in large shallow dish; add drumsticks, turning to coat all over with marinade. *[Best made ahead to this stage. Cover, refrigerate 3 hours or overnight.]*

Drain drumsticks over medium pan; reserve marinade. Cook drumsticks on heated oiled grill until browned all over. Cook in covered grill, using indirect heat, following manufacturer's instructions, about 15 minutes or until browned all over and tender.

Meanwhile, place reserved marinade on grill. Bring to boil; simmer, stirring, about 5 minutes or until thick. Serve satay sauce with drumsticks.

SERVES 4

STICKY BBQ CHICKEN

8 chicken thighs
3 tablespoons honey
1 clove garlic, crushed
1 teaspoon grated fresh ginger
1¹/₂ tablespoons soy sauce
1¹/₂ tablespoons sweet chili sauce

Place chicken in large shallow dish with combined honey, garlic, ginger and sauces. *[Best made ahead to this stage. Cover, refrigerate 3 hours or overnight.]*

Drain chicken over small bowl; reserve marinade. Place chicken on oiled roasting rack or basket, or in disposable baking dish, brush with reserved marinade. Cook chicken in covered grill, using indirect heat, following manufacturer's instructions, about 30 minutes or until browned on both sides and tender. Turn chicken after 15 minutes; brush with marinade.

SERVES 4

From left Drumsticks with crunchy satay sauce; Sticky bbq chicken

TANDOORI CHICKEN WITH CUCUMBER MINT RAITA

You need 8oz smoking chips for this recipe.

- **1/2 cup tandoori paste**
- **1 cup yogurt**
- **2 cloves garlic, crushed**
- **2 teaspoons grated fresh ginger**
- **31/2lb chicken**
- **1 cup green ginger wine**

CUCUMBER MINT RAITA

- **1 English cucumber**
- **1 cup yogurt**
- **3 tablespoons finely chopped fresh mint**
- **1/2 teaspoon ground cumin**
- **1/2 teaspoon ground coriander**

Combine paste, yogurt, garlic and ginger in large bowl, add chicken; using hands, rub tandoori mixture all over chicken. *[Best made ahead to this stage. Cover, refrigerate overnight or freeze.]*

Combine smoking chips and wine in small bowl; let stand 2 hours. Tuck chicken wings under body, tie legs together with kitchen string; place chicken on oiled roasting rack. Place drained smoking chips in smoke box; place alongside chicken on grill. Cook in covered grill, using indirect heat, following manufacturer's instructions, about 1 hour and 20 minutes or until browned all over and tender. Serve with Cucumber Mint Raita.

Cucumber Mint Raita Peel cucumber; halve lengthwise, discard seeds. Chop cucumber coarsely; combine in small bowl with remaining ingredients. Cover, refrigerate. *[Best made no more than 3 hours ahead of serving.]*

SERVES 4 TO 6

Left Tandoori chicken with cucumber mint raita
Above Turkey with raisin and Brazil nut stuffing

TURKEY WITH RAISIN AND BRAZIL NUT STUFFING

- **11/2 tablespoons butter**
- **1 medium onion, chopped**
- **11/4 cups Brazil nuts, chopped**
- **11/2 cups raisins, chopped**
- **7lb turkey**
- **3 tablespoons soy sauce**
- **11/2 tablespoons honey**

Heat butter in medium pan; cook onion, stirring, until soft. Remove from heat, stir in nuts and raisins.

Discard turkey neck and giblets. Rinse turkey under cold water; pat dry inside and out. Tuck wings under body; spoon raisin mixture into body cavity. Tuck trimmed neck flap under body, securing with toothpicks; tie legs together with kitchen string. Place turkey on roasting rack or basket, or in disposable baking dish. Brush with combined sauce and honey. Cook in covered grill, using indirect heat, following manufacturer's instructions, 21/2 hours or until browned all over and tender.

SERVES 6 TO 8

Setting from Accoutrement

CHICKEN WITH CARAMELIZED PEAR

4 skinless, boneless chicken breast halves
3 tablespoons butter
1/4 cup firmly packed brown sugar
3 large pears, peeled, sliced thickly
12 paper thin slices prosciutto

Cut each chicken breast in 3 strips diagonally; place each strip between pieces of plastic wrap, pound gently with meat mallet until just flattened.

Melt butter and sugar in medium pan on grill; cook pear, stirring, until pear caramelizes and sauce thickens. Meanwhile, cook chicken strips on heated oiled grill until browned on both sides and tender. Cook prosciutto on heated oiled grill until browned on both sides and crisp. Serve chicken with prosciutto and caramelized pear.

SERVES 4

ROSEMARY-SMOKED CHICKEN BREAST

You need 8oz smoking chips for this recipe.

1 clove garlic, crushed
1 1/2 cups dry white wine
1 1/2 tablespoons finely chopped fresh rosemary
4 skinless, boneless chicken breast halves
2 cups water
1 clove garlic, crushed, extra
3 tablespoons coarsely chopped fresh rosemary, extra
3 tablespoons olive oil
7oz oyster mushrooms
7oz enoki mushrooms
14oz baby spinach leaves

Combine garlic, 1/2 cup of the wine and finely chopped rosemary in large shallow dish; add chicken, mix well. *[Must be made ahead to this stage. Cover, refrigerate for 3 hours or overnight.]*

Combine water, remaining wine, extra garlic and extra rosemary in large bowl; add smoking chips, mix well. Let stand at least 2 hours or overnight.

Cook chicken on both sides on heated oiled grill 2 minutes on each side. Place chicken on oiled roasting rack or basket, or in disposable baking dish. Place drained smoking chips in smoke box; place alongside chicken on grill. Cook in covered grill, using indirect heat, following manufacturer's instructions, about 35 minutes or until browned all over and tender.

Just before serving, heat half the oil in wok; stir-fry oyster mushrooms about 3 minutes or until just tender, remove from wok. Heat remaining oil in wok; stir-fry enoki mushrooms and spinach only long enough to heat, not wilt. Serve chicken with spinach and mushrooms.

SERVES 4

Right Rosemary-smoked chicken breast
Above Chicken with caramelized pear

PORTUGUESE-STYLE SEARED POUSSIN

4 poussin
**1¹/₂ tablespoons cracked
   black pepper**
1¹/₂ tablespoons ground cumin
1¹/₂ tablespoons lemon juice
1¹/₂ tablespoons olive oil
¹/₂ teaspoon chili powder
¹/₂ teaspoon hot paprika
¹/₄ teaspoon cayenne pepper
1 clove garlic, crushed

Cut along both sides of each poussin backbone; discard backbones.

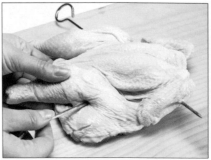

Insert metal skewer through thigh and opposite wing. Repeat with other thigh and wing.

Combine remaining ingredients in small bowl; mix to a smooth paste. Using hands, rub chili paste all over poussin pieces. Cook in covered grill, using indirect heat, following manufacturer's instructions, 20 minutes. Turn poussin; cook about 20 minutes or until browned all over and tender.

SERVES 4

POUSSIN WITH FENNEL

2 poussin
3 tablespoons butter
**1 medium fennel
   bulb, sliced**
¹/₄ cup Pernod

Cut along both sides of each poussin backbone; discard backbones. Place poussin, breast side up, on board; press breastbone to flatten poussin.

Heat butter in large pan; cook fennel, stirring, until soft and browned lightly; add Pernod; transfer mixture to disposable baking dish. Cook poussin on heated oiled grill until browned on both sides; place poussin on top of fennel mixture in dish. Cook poussin in covered grill, using indirect heat, following manufacturer's instructions, about 30 minutes or until browned all over and tender.

SERVES 2

Knife and fork from Accoutrement; basket, bowl and plate from Shack

ROASTED WHOLE CHICKEN WITH CARAMELIZED LEMON

3 tablespoons butter
2 medium lemons, sliced
4 small red onions, chopped
3¹/₂lb chicken
¹/₄ cup olive oil
¹/₄ cup lemon juice

Heat half the butter in medium pan; cook lemon, stirring, until just softened and caramelized slightly. Remove from pan; cool. Heat remaining butter in same pan; cook onion, stirring, until soft and browned lightly. Remove from pan; cool.

Push lemon between flesh and skin of chicken; spoon onion into body cavity. Tuck trimmed neck flap under body, securing with toothpicks; tie legs together with kitchen string. Place chicken on oiled roasting rack or basket, or in disposable baking dish. Brush all over with combined oil and juice. Cook chicken in covered grill, using indirect heat, following manufacturer's instructions, about 1 hour and 20 minutes or until browned all over and tender.

SERVES 4

Right, from top Portuguese-style seared poussin; Poussin with fennel
Above Roasted whole chicken with caramelized lemon

APRICOT CHICKEN

2 tablespoons butter
3 large yellow onions,
chopped
8oz ground chicken
1/4 cup chopped
dried apricots
1 cup fresh breadcrumbs
3 tablespoons cream
3 1/4lb boned chicken
1 1/2 tablespoons olive oil
2 cups apricot nectar

Heat butter in small pan; cook about a third of the onion, stirring, until just soft. Combine cooled onion in large bowl with the ground chicken, apricots, breadcrumbs and cream.

Open chicken out on flat surface, skin-side down; mound apricot filling mixture in center of chicken.

Roll chicken tightly; tie with kitchen string at 1 inch intervals. Place in oiled disposable baking dish. Cook in covered grill, using indirect heat, following manufacturer's instructions, for about 1 1/2 hours or until browned all over and tender. Remove chicken from dish, keep warm; reserve pan juices.

Heat oil in medium pan on grill; cook remaining onion, stirring, until browned. Add nectar and pan juices, bring to boil; simmer, uncovered, 5 minutes. Serve apricot sauce with chicken.

SERVES 4 TO 6

GRILLED POUSSIN WITH CITRUS FLAVORS

Game hens may be substituted for poussin, if desired

4 poussin
1/4 cup marmalade
1 1/2 tablespoons finely grated
lemon rind
1 1/2 tablespoons finely grated
lime rind
1 1/2 tablespoons lemon juice
1 1/2 tablespoons lime juice
1 1/2 tablespoons Grand Marnier
1 1/2 tablespoons chopped
fresh oregano
1 1/2 tablespoons cracked
black pepper
3 tablespoons olive oil

Cut along both sides of each poussin backbone; discard backbones. Cut each poussin in half between breasts. Combine remaining ingredients in large bowl; add poussin pieces, mix well. *[Best made ahead to this stage. Cover, refrigerate 3 hours or overnight.]*

Place poussin on heated oiled grill. Cover, cook, using indirect heat, following manufacturer's instructions, 20 minutes. Turn poussin, cook 20 minutes or until browned on both sides and tender.

SERVES 4

HOT HOT HOT CHICKEN WINGS

12 chicken wings
³/4 cup vegetable oil
2 cloves garlic, crushed
1¹/2 tablespoons hot paprika
1¹/2 tablespoons ground cumin
1¹/2 tablespoons ground turmeric
1¹/2 tablespoons ground coriander
1¹/2 tablespoons grated lime rind
2 teaspoons chili powder
2 teaspoons hot curry powder

Make 2 deep cuts in thickest part of each wing. Combine remaining ingredients in large bowl; add chicken wings, mix well. [Must be made ahead to this stage. Cover, refrigerate 3 hours or overnight.]

Cook wings on heated oiled grill, uncovered, until they are browned on both sides and tender.

SERVES 4

Left Apricot chicken
Above, from top Grilled poussin with citrus flavors; Hot hot hot chicken wings

VODKA AND SZECHUAN PEPPER GLAZED CHICKEN

1/2 cup sugar
1/2 cup lemon juice
1/4 cup vodka
11/2 tablespoons water
1 teaspoon roasted crushed
   Szechuan peppercorns
31/2lb chicken

BLINI

3 large potatoes
3 tablespoons peanut oil
2 small white onions,
   chopped finely
3 cloves garlic, crushed
11/2 cups self-rising flour
2 teaspoons sugar
2 eggs, beaten lightly
11/2 cups milk

Barbecue from Kangaroo TentCity & BBQ's

LIME CHICKEN ON LEMON GRASS SKEWERS

6 12-inch long fresh lemon
   grass stalks
1/3 cup peanut oil
11/2 tablespoons grated lime rind
1/4 cup coarsely chopped
   fresh cilantro
6 skinless, boneless chicken
   breast halves
1/4 cup lime juice
2 small hot red chilies, seeded,
   chopped finely
1/3 cup macadamia or olive oil
11/2 tablespoons raw sugar
1 clove garlic, crushed

Cut 1 inch off the end of each lemon grass stalk; reserve stalks. Chop the 1 inch pieces finely then combine in large shallow dish with peanut oil, rind and cilantro.

Cut each breast in 4 strips crosswise; thread 4 strips on each lemon grass stalk "skewer". Place skewers in dish, turning to coat chicken in lemon grass marinade. *[Must be made ahead to this stage. Cover, refrigerate 3 hours or overnight.]*

Cook skewers on heated oiled grill, uncovered, until chicken is browned all over and tender. Meanwhile, combine remaining ingredients in jar, shake well; serve with chicken skewers.

SERVES 6

Combine sugar, juice, vodka, water and pepper in small pan. Boil, uncovered, for about 5 minutes or until slightly thickened; divide glaze into two portions. Place chicken on roasting rack or basket. Cook in covered grill, using indirect heat, 1 hour. Brush chicken with one portion of glaze, cook 20 minutes more or until chicken is browned all over and tender. Just before serving, brush with remaining glaze. Serve chicken with blini.

Blini Boil, steam or microwave potatoes until tender; drain, mash. Heat oil in large pan, add onion and garlic; cook, stirring, until onion is soft. Combine mashed potato and onion mixture in large bowl with flour, sugar, eggs and milk. Cook 1/4 cup portions of potato mixture on heated oiled grill plate until browned on both sides and cooked through.

SERVES 4 TO 6

MARMALADE CHICKEN WITH ASPARAGUS WALNUT SALAD

1 cup orange marmalade
1/4 cup Grand Marnier
1/4 cup orange juice
31/2lb chicken

ASPARAGUS WALNUT SALAD
1lb asparagus
1/4 cup finely chopped walnuts, toasted
2 teaspoons stone ground mustard
11/2 tablespoons red wine vinegar
1 small shallot, chopped finely
1/4 cup extra virgin olive oil
4oz baby arugula

Combine marmalade, liqueur and juice in small pan. Bring to boil, simmer, uncovered, for about 5 minutes or until glaze thickens. Divide glaze into two portions. Place chicken on roasting rack or basket.

Cook in covered grill, using indirect heat, following manufacturer's instructions, 1 hour. Brush chicken with one portion of glaze, cook 20 minutes more or until browned all over and tender. Just before serving, brush chicken with remaining glaze. Serve chicken with Asparagus Walnut Salad.

Asparagus Walnut Salad Cut asparagus spears into 4 inch lengths. Boil, steam or microwave asparagus until tender. Blend or process half the walnuts with mustard, vinegar, shallot and oil until smooth. Just before serving, combine asparagus with arugula and walnut dressing, sprinkle with remaining walnuts.

SERVES 4 TO 6

Left Lime chicken on lemon grass skewers
Below, from left Marmalade chicken with asparagus walnut salad; Vodka and Szechuan pepper glazed chicken

MARJORAM AND ORANGE TURKEY

You need 3 small oranges for this recipe.

8lb turkey
2 small oranges, quartered
6 fresh bay leaves
2 sprigs fresh marjoram

ORANGE BUTTER
1/4 cup dry white wine
2 teaspoons finely grated orange rind
8 tablespoons butter, chopped
1 clove garlic, crushed
3 tablespoons brown sugar
3 tablespoons orange juice

Discard turkey neck and giblets. Rinse turkey under cold water; pat dry inside and out. Tuck wings under body; place oranges, bay leaves and marjoram loosely inside body cavity. Tuck trimmed neck flap under body, securing with toothpicks; tie legs together with kitchen string. Place turkey on oiled roasting rack or basket, or in disposable baking dish, brush with Orange Butter. Cook in covered grill, using indirect heat, following manufacturer's instructions, about 2 1/2 hours or until browned all over and tender; brush occasionally with Orange Butter, cover wings with foil if over-browning.

Orange Butter Combine all ingredients in small pan; cook, stirring, until combined and heated through.

SERVES 8

RED CURRANT-GLAZED DUCK

4lb duck
2 teaspoons olive oil
1 medium onion, chopped
3 tablespoons brown sugar
3 tablespoons red wine vinegar
1/3 cup orange juice
1/3 cup chicken stock
3 tablespoons red currant jelly
3 tablespoons flaked almonds, toasted

Place duck in disposable baking dish; cook in covered grill, using indirect heat, following manufacturer's instructions, 1 hour. Remove duck; using scissors, cut into 8 pieces. Discard fat then return duck pieces to dish.

Heat oil in small pan on grill; cook onion, stirring, until soft. Add sugar and vinegar; cook, stirring, until vinegar has almost evaporated. Add juice, stock and jelly to pan; cook, stirring, until jelly melts and mixture thickens slightly. Pour glaze over duck in dish, return to covered grill; cook about 30 minutes or until duck is browned all over and tender. Serve sprinkled with toasted flaked almonds, over grilled orange slices, if desired.

SERVES 4

Crab apple jelly may be substituted for red current jelly, if preferred.

Below Marjoram and orange turkey
Right, from top Duck with Madeira and juniper berries; Red currant-glazed duck

Barbecue from Barbeques Galore

DUCK WITH MADEIRA AND JUNIPER BERRIES

2 teaspoons dried juniper berries
1¹/₂ tablespoons Szechuan pepper
6 star anise
2 teaspoons salt
4lb duck
²/₃ cup Madeira

Crush or process berries, pepper, star anise and salt until powdered. Place duck in disposable baking dish, tuck wings under body, securing with toothpicks; tie legs together with kitchen string. Combine crushed juniper berry mixture with Madeira in small bowl; pour over duck. *[Best made ahead to this stage. Cover, refrigerate 3 hours or overnight.]*

Cook duck in covered grill, using indirect heat, following manufacturer's instructions, about 1 hour and 40 minutes or until browned all over and tender; brush occasionally with pan juices.

SERVES 4

Glasses from Wednesdays Value Homewares; plates and platter from Country Floors

QUAIL WITH PANCETTA AND SUN-DRIED BELL PEPPERS

2/3 cup peanut oil
3 tablespoons balsamic vinegar
3 tablespoons lemon juice
3 tablespoons soy sauce
1 1/2 tablespoons brown sugar
6 quail
12 paper-thin slices pancetta
1 cup sun-dried sweet bell peppers
    in oil, drained

Combine oil, vinegar, juice, sauce and sugar in large bowl; add quail, mix well. *[Must be made ahead to this stage. Cover, refrigerate 3 hours or overnight.]*

Drain quail over small pan; reserve marinade. Tie legs together with kitchen string; place quail in oiled roasting basket or disposable baking dish. Cook in covered grill, using indirect heat, following manufacturer's instructions, for 30 minutes or until browned and tender.

Meanwhile, cook pancetta on heated oiled grill until browned and crisp. Place reserved marinade on grill, bring to boil; simmer, whisking, 2 minutes. Serve quail with the bell peppers, pancetta and hot marinade.

SERVES 4

QUAIL GRILLED NORTH-AFRICAN STYLE

1/2 cup couscous
1/2 cup boiling water
11/2 tablespoons olive oil
1 small white onion,
   finely chopped
2 cloves garlic, crushed
2 teaspoons ground cumin
2 teaspoons ground coriander
2 green onions, chopped
1/4 cup dried currants
1/4 cup dried apricots, sliced
3 tablespoons finely chopped
   fresh cilantro
3 tablespoons finely chopped
   fresh mint
12 quail

CUMIN DRESSING

3 tablespoons olive oil
11/2 tablespoons lemon juice
1 teaspoon cumin seeds
1 clove garlic, crushed
1/4 teaspoon sugar

Combine couscous and the boiling water in medium heatproof bowl; cover, stand for about 5 minutes or until the water is absorbed.

Meanwhile, heat oil in large pan; cook white onion, garlic and spices, stirring, until onion is soft. Using a fork, toss couscous, green onion, fruit and herbs into spice mixture. *[Can be made ahead to this stage. Cover, refrigerate overnight.]*

Rinse quail under cold water; pat dry inside and out. Tuck wings under body, securing with toothpicks. Spoon couscous mixture into body cavity, securing opening with toothpicks. Secure legs with kitchen string; place quail directly on oiled grill or plate. Cook in covered grill, using indirect heat, following manufacturer's instructions, for about 20 minutes or until browned all over and tender. Drizzle with Cumin Dressing.

Cumin Dressing Whisk all ingredients together in small bowl.

SERVES 4 TO 6

LIME AND GREEN PEPPERCORN QUAIL

12 quail
1/2 cup olive oil
1/4 cup drained green peppercorns,
   crushed
3 tablespoons finely grated
   lime rind
1/2 cup lime juice
2 cloves garlic, crushed
3 tablespoons finely chopped
   fresh cilantro

Plate, cutlery and tea-towel from Accoutrement

Cut along both sides of each quail backbone; discard backbones. Cut each quail in half along breastbone. Combine remaining ingredients in large bowl; add quail pieces, mix well. *[Best made ahead to this stage. Cover, refrigerate for 3 hours or overnight.]*

Drain quail over small bowl; reserve marinade. Cook quail on heated oiled grill, brushing frequently with reserved marinade, about 5 minutes each side or until browned all over and tender.

SERVES 4 TO 6

CHICKEN TIKKA WITH GRILLED BANANAS

1/3 cup tikka curry paste
1/2 cup yogurt
2 cloves garlic, crushed
2 teaspoons grated fresh ginger
11/2 tablespoons chopped
   fresh cilantro
1 teaspoon ground coriander
1 teaspoon ground cumin
31/2lb chicken

GRILLED BANANAS

4 medium bananas
1 small hot red chili, chopped finely
1 teaspoon finely grated lime rind
1/2 cup coconut milk

Combine paste, yogurt, garlic, ginger, cilantro, ground coriander, and cumin in large bowl. Add chicken; using hands, rub tikka mixture all over chicken. *[Must be made ahead. Cover, refrigerate overnight.]*

Place chicken on oiled roasting rack or basket, or in disposable baking dish. Cook in covered grill, using indirect heat, following manufacturer's instructions, about 1 hour and 20 minutes or until browned all over and tender. Serve with Grilled Bananas.

Grilled Bananas Cut unpeeled bananas in half lengthwise; cut each half into 2 pieces. Combine chili, rind and milk in small bowl. Brush a little of the mixture over cut side of each banana. Cook banana on heated oiled grill until browned and soft. Drizzle banana with remaining milk mixture, if desired.

SERVES 4 TO 6

Left, from bottom Lime and green peppercorn quail; Quail grilled North-African style; Quail with pancetta and sun-dried bell peppers *Above* Chicken tikka with grilled bananas

Lamb

Lamb grills to juicy perfection, marrying happily with the flavors of many cuisines from around the world. Try lamb with black sesame seed dressing, for instance, or lamb with garlic and shiitake mushrooms. For the best results, don't overcook lamb – the meat should be moist and pink on the inside. And, for added succulence, allow larger cuts to rest in a warm place for at least 15 minutes before carving.

MINI ROAST WITH HORSERADISH CREAM

Mini lamb roasts are cut from the round of the leg ad weigh 6-7oz each.

1/3 cup red currant jelly
1/4 cup olive oil
4 mini lamb roasts
5 medium red potatoes
10 cloves garlic, unpeeled
3 tablespoons sea salt
1/4 cup hazelnut oil
1/4 cup grated fresh horseradish
1 1/2 cups creme fraiche

Combine jelly and olive oil in large bowl, add lamb; mix well. *[Best made ahead to this stage. Cover, refrigerate 3 hours or overnight.]*

Cut each potato into 8 wedges. Combine potato, garlic, salt and hazelnut oil in disposable baking dish. Cook in covered grill, using indirect heat, following manufacturer's instructions, 35 minutes.

Remove grill cover, cook lamb on heated oiled grill until browned all over. Replace cover, cook, using indirect heat, about 10 minutes or until lamb is cooked as desired.

Serve lamb and potato wedges with combined horseradish and creme fraiche.

SERVES 4

LEMON AND ARTICHOKE RACK OF LAMB

2 racks of lamb with 8 chops each
2 medium yellow onions, sliced
1 medium lemon
14 1/2 oz can artichoke hearts, drained, quartered
3 tablespoons drained capers
2 tablespoons butter
1 teaspoon brown sugar

Cook lamb and onion on heated oiled grill plate until lamb is browned all over and onion soft. Cut lemon into 8 wedges. Place lamb, onion and lemon in disposable baking dish with remaining ingredients. Cook in covered grill, using indirect heat, following manufacturer's instructions, about 30 minutes or until lamb is cooked as desired.

SERVES 4

Right, from top Mini roast with horseradish cream; Lemon and artichoke rack of lamb

LAMB ROASTS WITH CITRUS TABBOULEH

- **3 tablespoons sumac [see Glossary] or tamarind concentrate**
- **3 tablespoons olive oil**
- **1 clove garlic, crushed**
- **4 mini lamb roasts**
- **8oz yogurt**

CITRUS TABBOULEH

- **1/2 cup bulghur**
- **1 cup coarsely chopped Italian parsley**
- **6 small tomatoes, seeded, chopped finely**
- **3 tablespoons coarsely chopped fresh mint**
- **3 tablespoons coarsely chopped fresh basil**
- **3 tablespoons grated lemon rind**
- **3 tablespoons lemon juice**
- **2 cloves garlic, crushed**
- **1 teaspoon cracked black pepper**

Combine sumac or tamarind, oil and garlic in large shallow dish, add lamb; mix well. *[Best made ahead. Cover, refrigerate for 3 hours or overnight.]*

Cook lamb, uncovered, on heated oiled grill until browned all over and cooked as desired. Serve lamb with yogurt and Citrus Tabbouleh.

Citrus Tabbouleh Place bulghur in small bowl, cover with cold water, stand 15 minutes; drain. Rinse bulghur under cold water, drain; squeeze to remove excess moisture. Combine bulghur in medium bowl with remaining ingredients. *[Best made just before serving.]*

SERVES 4

RED WINE LAMB WITH GARLIC POTATOES

- **1 cup dry red wine**
- **1/4 cup finely chopped fresh rosemary**
- **2 cloves garlic, crushed**
- **4lb leg of lamb**
- **1/4 cup stone ground mustard**
- **1/4 cup finely chopped fresh mint**

GARLIC POTATOES

- **8 medium potatoes**
- **2 cloves garlic, crushed**
- **7 tablespoons butter, melted**

Combine wine, rosemary and garlic in large shallow dish, add lamb. *[Best made ahead. Cover, refrigerate for 3 hours or overnight.]*

Drain lamb; discard marinade. Place lamb on roasting rack or basket, or in disposable baking dish. Cook in covered

GARLIC AND ROSEMARY SMOKED LAMB

You need 8oz smoking chips for this recipe.

- **2lb boned, rolled lamb loin**
- **4 cloves garlic, halved**
- **8 fresh rosemary sprigs**
- **1 teaspoon dried chili flakes**
- **1 1/2 tablespoons olive oil**

Place lamb in large bowl. Pierce lamb in 8 places with sharp knife; push garlic halves and rosemary sprigs into cuts.

Sprinkle lamb with chili; rub with oil. *[Best made ahead. Cover, refrigerate for 3 hours or overnight.]*

Soak smoking chips in large bowl of water 2 hours.

Cook lamb, uncovered, on heated oiled grill until browned all over. Place drained chips in smoke box on grill next to lamb. Cook lamb in covered grill, using indirect heat, following manufacturer's instructions, for about 40 minutes or until cooked as desired.

SERVES 4 TO 6

grill, using indirect heat, following manufacturer's instructions, 1 hour. Spread lamb with mustard, sprinkle with mint; cook, covered, about 15 minutes or until cooked as desired. Serve lamb with Garlic Potatoes.

Garlic Potatoes Wrap potatoes individually in foil; cook in covered grill, using indirect heat, following manufacturer's instructions, about 45 minutes or until tender. Place potatoes on flat surface; hit with a meat mallet to flatten. Just before serving, remove foil; brush potatoes with combined garlic and butter.

SERVES 4 TO 6

Left Garlic and rosemary smoked lamb
Above Lamb roasts with citrus tabbouleh
Right Red wine lamb with garlic potatoes

MINTED LAMB WITH BABY BEET AND ARUGULA SALAD

1/4 cup olive oil
2 cloves garlic, crushed
1/2 cup chopped fresh mint
2 racks of lamb with 8 chops each
1 1/2 tablespoons olive oil, extra
1/4 cup chopped fresh mint, extra

BABY BEET AND ARUGULA SALAD
2lb bunch baby beets
1 medium lemon
8oz arugula
3 tablespoons olive oil

3 tablespoons raspberry vinegar
1/4 cup parmesan, shaved

Combine oil, garlic and mint in large shallow dish; add lamb, mix well. [Best made ahead. Cover, refrigerate for 3 hours or overnight.]

Drain lamb; discard marinade. Place lamb on roasting rack or basket, or in disposable baking dish. Cook in covered grill, using indirect heat, following manufacturer's instructions, 25 minutes.

Brush top of lamb with extra oil, sprinkle with extra mint; cook, covered, about 10 minutes or until cooked as desired. Remove from heat, cover; let stand 10 minutes before serving with Baby Beet and Arugula Salad.

Baby Beet and Arugula Salad Cut beet stems 1-inch from top of beets; remove and discard roots. Wrap beets in foil, cook next to lamb on heated grill 10 minutes or until tender; remove from foil. Remove skin from beets. Peel rind thinly from lemon, avoiding any white pith; cut rind into thin strips. Place arugula and beets in medium bowl, drizzle with combined oil and vinegar, sprinkle with lemon rind. Scatter parmesan over salad.

SERVES 4

LAMB WITH GARLIC AND SHIITAKE MUSHROOMS

12 cloves garlic, peeled
1¹/₂ tablespoons sugar
¹/₄ cup olive oil
3 lamb eye of loin
14oz shiitake mushrooms, halved
3 tablespoons butter, melted
3 tablespoons chopped fresh chives

Combine garlic, sugar and 3 tablespoons of the oil in disposable baking dish. Cook in covered grill, using indirect heat, following manufacturer's instructions, about 15 minutes or until garlic is soft and slightly caramelized. Remove from grill; cover to keep warm.

Brush lamb with remaining oil; cook, uncovered, on heated oiled grill until browned all over and cooked as desired.

Meanwhile, toss mushrooms, butter and chives together in a large bowl. Transfer mushroom mixture to heated oiled grill plate; cook until tender. Serve lamb with roasted garlic and mushrooms.

SERVES 4 TO 6

Above, from top Minted lamb with baby beet and arugula salad; Lamb with garlic and shiitake mushrooms

MUSTARD LAMB RIB CHOPS WITH BASIL CREAM

2 racks of lamb with 8 chops each
1/2 cup olive oil
1/2 cup coarsely chopped
    fresh basil
1 clove garlic, crushed
2lb fingerling potatoes
1 1/2 tablespoons olive oil, extra
2 tablespoons stone ground mustard

BASIL CREAM

2 teaspoons olive oil
1 medium white onion, sliced finely
1 clove garlic, crushed
1/2 cup dry white wine
1 1/4 cups cream
1/2 cup coarsely chopped
    fresh basil

Cut lamb racks into double chops. Combine oil, basil and garlic in large shallow dish, add chops; mix well. *[Best made ahead. Cover, refrigerate 3 hours or overnight.]*

Cut potatoes in half lengthwise, brush with extra oil; place in disposable baking dish. Cook in covered grill, using indirect heat, following manufacturer's instructions, about 45 minutes or until potatoes are softened; keep warm.

Drain chops; discard marinade. Cook chops, uncovered, on heated oiled grill until browned all over and cooked as desired. Spread with mustard, serve with Basil Cream and potatoes.

Basil Cream Heat oil in medium pan on grill, cook onion and garlic, stirring, until soft. Add wine, simmer, uncovered, 5 minutes or until reduced by half. Add cream; boil 5 minutes or until sauce thickens. Remove from heat, stir in basil; serve immediately.

SERVES 4 TO 6

LAMB AND ARTICHOKE KEBABS

Soak bamboo skewers in water for about 1 hour to prevent them from scorching.

2lb diced lamb
2 14 1/2 oz cans artichoke hearts,
    drained, halved
1 sweet red bell pepper, chopped
12oz button mushrooms, halved

GARLIC BASIL DRESSING

1/2 cup red wine vinegar
1/4 cup olive oil
1 1/2 tablespoons shredded
    fresh basil
1 clove garlic, crushed
1 teaspoon sugar
1 teaspoon Dijon mustard

Thread lamb, artichoke hearts, peppers and mushrooms on 8 large skewers. [Can be made a day ahead to this stage. Cover, refrigerate overnight.]

Cook kebabs, in batches, on heated oiled grill until browned all over and cooked as desired.

Serve with Garlic Basil Dressing.

Garlic Basil Dressing Combine all the ingredients in a jar; shake well.

SERVES 4

MINTED BUTTERFLIED LEG OF LAMB

3lb butterflied leg of lamb
1 cup dry white wine
3 cloves garlic, crushed
1/4 cup chopped fresh mint
1/4 cup chopped fresh parsley
3 tablespoons soy sauce
1 1/2 tablespoons brown sugar

Combine lamb with remaining ingredients in disposable baking dish. [Best made ahead. Cover, refrigerate overnight.]

Cook lamb in covered grill, using indirect heat, following manufacturer's instructions, about 50 minutes or until cooked as desired. During cooking, brush lamb occasionally with pan juices.

SERVES 4 TO 6

Above, from top Lamb and artichoke kebabs; Minted butterflied leg of lamb
Left Mustard lamb rib chops with basil cream

MINT AND LIME LAMB WITH SALSA

1/2 cup olive oil
2 cloves garlic, crushed
2 teaspoons grated lime rind
3 tablespoons lime juice
3 tablespoons chopped fresh mint
8 lamb chops

WATERMELON AND MANGO SALSA
4 cups chopped watermelon
3 small mangoes, chopped
2 small red chilies,
   seeded, chopped
1/4 cup shredded fresh cilantro
3 tablespoons grated lime rind
1/4 cup raspberry vinegar

Combine oil, garlic, rind, juice and mint in medium bowl, add chops; mix well. *[Best made ahead to this stage. Cover, refrigerate 3 hours or overnight.]*

Cook chops, uncovered, on heated oiled grill until browned on both sides and cooked as desired. Serve with Watermelon and Mango Salsa.

Watermelon and Mango Salsa Combine all ingredients in large bowl; cover, then refrigerate 3 hours.

SERVES 4

Above Mint and lime lamb with salsa
Right, clockwise from top Beet and yogurt dip; Minted pesto; Indian chutney; Raita; Red onion and balsamic jam

Serve these accompaniments with loin or French rib chops from the grill.

RAITA

1 cup yogurt
1/2 English cucumber, seeded, chopped finely
1 teaspoon cumin seeds, toasted
1 clove garlic, crushed
1 1/2 tablespoons lemon juice

Combine all ingredients in small bowl.
MAKES ABOUT 1 CUP

INDIAN CHUTNEY

1 1/2 cups cider vinegar
3/4 cup firmly packed brown sugar
1 medium yellow onion, chopped
14 1/2 oz can tomatoes
16oz can crushed pineapple
2 cups mixed dried fruit
1 1/2 tablespoons chopped candied ginger
1 clove garlic, crushed
1 1/2 tablespoons ground cumin
1 1/2 tablespoons ground coriander
2 teaspoons ground cloves
1 cinnamon stick

Combine all ingredients in large pan. Cook, stirring, over low heat until sugar is dissolved. Bring to boil; simmer, uncovered, stirring occasionally, for about 1 hour or until thickened. Store covered, in refrigerator.

MAKES ABOUT 3 CUPS

MINTED PESTO

1 cup fresh mint
1/2 cup olive oil
3 tablespoons grated parmesan cheese
2 cloves garlic, crushed
3 tablespoons pine nuts, toasted

Blend or process all ingredients until smooth. Store, covered, in refrigerator.
MAKES ABOUT 3/4 CUP

BEET AND YOGURT DIP

8 1/4 oz can beet slices, drained
1/4 cup yogurt
1 1/2 tablespoons chopped fresh cilantro
1 clove garlic, crushed
1 teaspoon ground cumin

Blend or process all ingredients until smooth. Store, covered, in refrigerator.
MAKES ABOUT 1 CUP

RED ONION AND BALSAMIC JAM

1/4 cup olive oil
3 medium red onions, sliced
1/4 cup firmly packed brown sugar
1/3 cup balsamic vinegar
1/2 teaspoon dill seeds
1/4 cup chicken stock

Heat oil in pan; cook onion, stirring, until soft and browned lightly. Stir in sugar, vinegar, seeds and stock. Simmer, uncovered, about 20 minutes or until mixture is thickened.

MAKES ABOUT 1 1/2 CUPS

LAMB WITH BLACK SESAME SEED DRESSING

1/3 cup soy sauce
1/3 cup oyster sauce
1/3 cup sweet chili sauce
1/4 cup water
3 cloves garlic, crushed
3 lamb eye of loin
1/4 cup black sesame seeds

POTATO ALMOND ROSTI

4 medium potatoes, grated finely
1 cup grated
  mozzarella cheese
1/2 cup finely ground almonds
1/3 cup finely chopped chives
1/3 cup finely chopped almonds
3 tablespoons sumac [see Glossary]
  or tamarind concentrate

Combine sauces, water and garlic in large bowl, add lamb; mix well. *[Best made ahead to this stage. Cover, refrigerate 3 hours or overnight.]*

Drain lamb over small pan; reserve marinade. Cook lamb, uncovered, on heated oiled grill until cooked as desired. Add sesame seeds to marinade. Bring to boil on grill, simmer for 2 minutes or until thickened slightly. Serve lamb with black sesame seed dressing and Potato Almond Rosti.

Potato Almond Rosti Combine potato with remaining ingredients in medium bowl. Spread 1/4 cup portions of mixture on heated oiled grill plate; cook until browned on both sides and crisp.

SERVES 4

BLACK BEAN LAMBURGERS

3 tablespoons salted black beans
1lb ground lamb
11/2 tablespoons chopped
  fresh cilantro
1 cup fresh breadcrumbs
1 egg, beaten lightly
3 medium tomatoes, chopped
1 small red onion, chopped
11/2 tablespoons peanut oil
4 crusty bread rolls
1 cup shredded lettuce leaves

Rinse beans under cold water 1 minute, drain; mash in large bowl. Add lamb, cilantro, breadcrumbs and egg. Shape mixture into 4 patties. *[Best made ahead. Cover, refrigerate 3 hours or overnight.]*

Combine tomato, onion and oil in small bowl. Cook patties, uncovered, on heated oiled grill until browned on both sides and cooked through. Split rolls; toast. Sandwich patties, tomato mixture and lettuce between roll halves.

MAKES 4

LAMB AND BULGHUR SAUSAGES

1/2 cup bulghur
11/2lb ground lamb
1/4 cup chopped fresh parsley
3 tablespoons chopped
   fresh mint
11/2 tablespoons finely grated
   lemon rind
2 medium tomatoes,
   peeled, chopped
11/2 tablespoons ground cumin
11/2 tablespoons ground coriander
2 cloves garlic, crushed
1/2 cup fresh breadcrumbs
1 egg, beaten lightly
2 large yellow onions, sliced
1 cup sour cream

Place bulghur in small bowl, cover with cold water, stand 15 minutes; drain. Rinse bulghur under cold water, drain; squeeze to remove excess moisture.

Combine bulghur in large bowl with lamb, herbs, rind, tomato, cumin, coriander, garlic, breadcrumbs and egg. Using hands, shape 1/4 cup portions of mixture into sausages. *[Best made ahead. Cover, refrigerate 3 hours or overnight.]*

Cook sausages, in batches, on heated oiled grill, until browned all over and cooked through. Meanwhile, cook onion on heated grill until browned. Serve sausages with sour cream.

SERVES 4 TO 6

BUTTERMILK LAMB SAUSAGES WITH ONION JAM

2lb ground lamb
1/2 cup buttermilk
3 tablespoons chopped
   fresh tarragon
2 small hot red chilies, chopped
2 cloves garlic, crushed

ONION JAM

2 tablespoons butter
3 large yellow onions,
   sliced thinly
3/4 cup brown malt vinegar
1/3 cup raw sugar

Combine lamb, buttermilk, tarragon, chili and garlic in large bowl. *[Best made ahead. Cover, refrigerate at least 1 hour.]*

Using hands, shape 1/4 cup portions of mixture into sausages. Cook sausages on heated oiled grill until browned all over and cooked through. Serve sausages with Onion Jam.

Onion Jam Melt butter in large pan; cook onion, vinegar and sugar over low heat, stirring occasionally, about 40 minutes or until mixture caramelizes.

SERVES 4 TO 6

Left Lamb with black sesame seed dressing
Above, from left Lamb and bulghur sausages;
Buttermilk lamb sausages with onion jam;
Black bean lamburgers

TANDOORI LAMB WITH INDIAN RICE STUFFING

You will need to cook about 1/3 cup raw rice for this recipe.

2 teaspoons vegetable oil
1 small white
   onion, chopped
1 clove garlic, crushed
2 teaspoons black mustard seeds
2 teaspoons cumin seeds
1 teaspoon ground coriander
1 cup cooked basmati rice
1/2 cup fresh breadcrumbs
1 egg, beaten lightly
11/2 tablespoons lemon juice
21/2lb boned lamb shoulder
1/2 cup yogurt
3 tablespoons tandoori paste

Heat oil in medium pan; cook onion and garlic, stirring, until onion is soft. Add seeds and coriander; cook, stirring, until seeds begin to pop. Combine spice mixture in medium bowl with rice, breadcrumbs, egg and juice. *[Can be made ahead to this stage. Cover, refrigerate overnight.]*

Fill cavity of lamb with rice stuffing; roll to enclose filling, tie with kitchen string. Brush lamb with combined yogurt and paste; place in disposable baking dish. Cook in covered grill, using indirect heat, following manufacturer's instructions, about 2 hours or until cooked as desired. Remove from heat, cover; stand 10 minutes before slicing and serving.

SERVES 4 TO 6

INDIAN SPICED LAMB WITH POTATO CAKES

1/4 cup yogurt
1/4 cup tandoori paste
1/4 cup lime juice
3 cloves garlic, crushed
11/2 tablespoons grated fresh ginger
11/2 tablespoons garam masala
3 lamb eye of loin

POTATO CAKES
3 medium potatoes
2 tablespoons butter
3/4 cup sour cream
1/3 cup self-rising flour
1/2 teaspoon baking powder

Combine yogurt, paste, juice, garlic, ginger and garam masala in large bowl, add lamb; mix well. [Best made ahead. Cover, refrigerate overnight.]

Remove lamb from marinade; discard marinade. Cook lamb, uncovered, on heated oiled grill until cooked as desired. Serve lamb with potato cakes.

Potato Cakes Boil, steam or microwave potatoes until tender; drain. Mash potato, stir in remaining ingredients; mix well. Using hands, shape 1/4 cup portions of mixture into patties; cook, in batches, on heated oiled grill plate until browned on both sides.

SERVES 4

CROWN ROAST WITH WILD RICE STUFFING

1/2 cup white and
    wild rice blend
1/4 cup olive oil
1 small white onion,
    chopped finely
2 cloves garlic, crushed
6 thin slices prosciutto, chopped

2 teaspoons chopped fresh rosemary
2 crown roasts of lamb (18 chops in
    2 separate pieces)
3 tablespoons red wine vinegar
1 1/2 tablespoons Dijon mustard

Cook rice in large pan of boiling water, uncovered, about 12 minutes or until just tender; drain. Heat 1 1/2 tablespoons of the oil in medium pan; cook onion, garlic and prosciutto, stirring, until onion is soft. Stir in rice and rosemary. [Can be made ahead. Cover, refrigerate overnight.]

Tie lamb pieces together with kitchen string to resemble a crown. Carefully

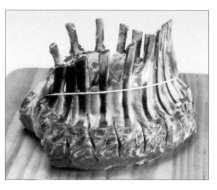

remove any skin or fat from bones at top. Place lamb roast in disposable baking dish or on large sheet of foil. Combine remaining oil, vinegar and mustard in bowl; brush half of mixture over lamb. Place a small heatproof bowl in center of roast to hold crown shape. Cover a disposable baking dish with foil or gather foil around to cover roast completely. Cook in covered grill, using indirect heat, following manufacturer's instructions, 20 minutes.

Remove foil and heatproof bowl from center of roast; spoon rice mixture into center. Wrap any extra stuffing in foil and place alongside roast. Brush roast with remaining oil mixture. Cook, in covered grill, using indirect heat, about 30 minutes or until cooked as desired.

SERVES 4 TO 6

Left, from top Tandoori lamb with Indian rice stuffing; Indian spiced lamb with potato cakes
Below Crown roast with wild rice stuffing

ROSEMARY LAMB SKEWERS WITH SPICED YOGURT

Soak bamboo skewers in water for about 1 hour to prevent them from scorching.

2lb lamb, cubed
1/4 cup light olive oil
1 cup dry red wine
3 tablespoons soy sauce
2 cloves garlic, crushed
3 tablespoons chopped fresh rosemary
1 teaspoon freshly ground black pepper
1 large red onion, chopped finely

SPICED YOGURT

1 cup yogurt
1 1/2 tablespoons lemon juice
2 teaspoons ground cumin
1 teaspoon sugar

Place lamb in large shallow dish, add remaining ingredients, mix well. *[Best made ahead to this stage. Cover, refrigerate 3 hours or overnight.]*

Drain lamb; discard marinade. Thread lamb on 8 skewers; cook, uncovered, on heated oiled grill until browned all over and cooked as desired. Serve lamb with Spiced Yogurt.

Spiced Yogurt Combine all ingredients in small bowl. *[Best made ahead; cover, refrigerate 1 hour or overnight.]*

SERVES 4

LAMB WITH PISTACHIO HARISSA AND COUSCOUS

8 large red chilies, chopped
4 cloves garlic, chopped
1 1/2 tablespoons ground cumin
1 1/2 tablespoons ground coriander
2 teaspoons grated lemon rind
1 1/2 tablespoons lemon juice
1/4 cup shelled pistachios
1 1/2 tablespoons chopped fresh mint
1 1/2 tablespoon chopped fresh cilantro
3 tablespoons olive oil
12 lamb rib chops

COUSCOUS

1 cup couscous
1 cup boiling water
1 1/2 tablespoons olive oil
3 tablespoons sliced dried apricots
1 1/2 tablespoons finely chopped fresh Italian parsley
3 tablespoons shelled chopped pistachios

Blend or process chili, garlic, spices, rind, juice, nuts, leaves and oil until pureed. Place chops in large shallow dish; spread with half the harissa. *[Best made ahead to this stage. Cover, refrigerate 3 hours, or overnight.]*

Cook chops, uncovered, on heated oiled grill until browned on both sides and cooked as desired. Serve chops with remaining harissa and Couscous.

Couscous Combine couscous and the water in medium heatproof bowl; cover, let stand about 5 minutes or until water is absorbed. Using fork, fluff couscous gently; toss in remaining ingredients.

SERVES 4

Left, from top Rosemary lamb skewers with spiced yogurt; Lamb with pistachio harissa and couscous
Above Tomato and mozzarella lamb stacks

TOMATO AND BOCCONCINI LAMB STACKS

2 teaspoons olive oil
3 tablespoons balsamic vinegar
2 cloves garlic, crushed
24 French-trimmed lamb rib chops
3 large plum tomatoes, sliced
10 1/2 oz bocconcini or baby mozzarella cheese, sliced
3 tablespoons coarsely chopped fresh basil

Combine oil, vinegar and garlic in small bowl; brush over chops. Cook chops, uncovered, on heated oiled grill until brown on one side; remove, place on oven tray, cooked-side up. Layer tomato, cheese and basil on cooked side of 12 chops; top with remaining 12 chops, cooked-side down. Tie chops together with kitchen string; return to grill. Cook until browned on both sides and cooked as desired.

SERVES 4 TO 6

Seafood

Seafood extravaganzas are a favorite for family get-togethers or special-occasion entertaining especially if you are lucky enough to live near the coast. Firm-fleshed fish are the best choice for the grill – select whole fish or thick steaks for best results – and don't forget the wonderful appeal of grilled calamari and shrimp or prawns.

BALSAMIC-FLAVORED OCTOPUS

3lb baby octopus
2 cloves garlic, crushed
1/4 cup olive oil
1/4 cup balsamic vinegar
1 1/2 tablespoons brown sugar
2 teaspoons chopped fresh thyme
5oz curly endive
3 tablespoons olive oil, extra
3 tablespoons balsamic vinegar, extra

Remove and discard heads and beaks from octopus; cut each octopus in half, combine in large bowl with garlic, oil, vinegar, sugar and thyme. *[Best made ahead to this stage. Cover, refrigerate 3 hours, overnight or freeze.]*

Drain octopus over small bowl; reserve marinade. Just before serving, cook octopus, in batches, on heated oiled grill, uncovered, until browned all over and just cooked through, brushing occasionally with reserved marinade. Serve with curly endive, drizzled with combined extra oil and extra vinegar.

SERVES 4 TO 6

SWORDFISH WITH TAPENADE

7oz black olives, pitted
1/4 cup drained capers
1/3 cup finely chopped fresh dill
1/3 cup finely chopped fresh Italian parsley
2 cloves garlic, crushed
3 tablespoons lemon juice
4 swordfish steaks

Blend or process olives, capers, dill, parsley, garlic and juice until almost a smooth paste. *[Best made ahead to this stage. Cover, refrigerate up to 3 days.]*

Cook steaks on heated oiled grill, uncovered, until browned on both sides and just cooked through; spread tops with tapenade.

SERVES 4

Tapenade is a zesty olive paste or spread of provincial origin

From top Balsamic-flavored octopus; Swordfish with tapenade

SEAFOOD BROCHETTES WITH LIME AND COCONUT

Soak bamboo skewers in water for about 1 hour to prevent them from scorching. You need 24 skewers for this recipe.

- **1lb piece tuna**
- **1lb piece salmon**
- **1lb piece swordfish**
- **1/3 cup jaggery [see Glossary] or brown sugar**
- **14oz can coconut milk**
- **3 tablespoons grated kaffir lime rind**
- **1/4 cup kaffir lime juice**
- **2 small hot red chilies, seeded, chopped finely**

Remove any skin from fish; cut each fish into 1¹/₂ inch pieces. Place sugar and milk in small pan; stir over low heat, without boiling, until sugar dissolves, cool. Stir in rind, juice, chili and fish. *[Best made ahead to this stage. Cover, refrigerate for 3 hours, overnight or freeze.]*

Drain fish over small pan; reserve marinade. Thread a mixture of fish pieces onto 12 pairs of skewers; grill on heated oiled grill, uncovered, until browned lightly and just cooked through. Place reserved marinade on grill; simmer, uncovered, 1 minute or until thickened slightly. Serve with brochettes.

MAKES 12

BLACKENED FISH FILLETS WITH SWEET TOMATO RELISH

- **4 thick white-fleshed fish fillets**
- **3 tablespoons olive oil**
- **3 tablespoons grated fresh ginger**
- **2 tablespoons ground turmeric**
- **1¹/₂ tablespoons garlic powder**
- **1¹/₂ tablespoons mustard powder**
- **1¹/₂ tablespoons sweet paprika**
- **1¹/₂ tablespoons dried basil**
- **1¹/₂ tablespoons ground fennel**
- **1/4 teaspoon cayenne pepper**
- **1/4 teaspoon hot chili powder**
- **2 teaspoons salt**

SWEET TOMATO RELISH
- **10 medium plum tomatoes, halved**
- **2 cups water**
- **1/2 cup dry white wine**
- **1¹/₂ tablespoons lime juice**
- **1/2 cup firmly packed brown sugar**
- **1¹/₂ tablespoons grated lime rind**
- **1¹/₂ tablespoons ground turmeric**
- **1¹/₂ tablespoons yellow mustard seeds**
- **2 bay leaves**
- **2 stalks fresh lemon grass**

Place fish in large shallow dish; pour over combined oil and ginger. *[Best made ahead to this stage. Cover, refrigerate for 3 hours or overnight.]*

Drain fish; discard marinade. Coat fish in combined remaining ingredients; cook on heated oiled grill, uncovered, until browned on both sides and just cooked through. Serve with Sweet Tomato Relish.

Sweet Tomato Relish Combine all ingredients in medium saucepan. Simmer, uncovered, 30 minutes or until most of the liquid has evaporated. Cool, remove and discard leaves and lemon grass. *[Best made ahead. Cover, refrigerate up to 1 week.]*

SERVES 4

Plate, sushi plate and small cup from Dinosaur Designs

SEAFOOD PLATTER

1lb baby octopus
1lb medium uncooked shrimp
or prawns
12 scallops in shells
12oz calamari rings
12oz firm white boneless
fish, chopped
12oz piece salmon
1/2 cup olive oil
1/4 cup balsamic vinegar
1/4 cup chopped drained
sun-dried tomatoes
3 tablespoons chopped
fresh oregano
2 cloves garlic, crushed
1 1/2 tablespoons lime juice
3 uncooked rock lobsters, halved
12 small blue mussels

Remove and discard heads and beaks from octopus; cut each octopus into quarters. Shell and devein shrimp or prawns, leaving tails intact. Remove scallops from shells; reserve shells. Combine octopus, shrimp or prawns, scallops, calamari and fish in large bowl with oil, vinegar, tomatoes, oregano, garlic and juice; mix well. [*Best made ahead. Cover, refrigerate for 3 hours or overnight.*]

Remove octopus, scallops, calamari, fish and salmon from marinade. Cook in batches, on heated oiled grill, uncovered, until browned all over and just cooked through. Slice salmon.

Remove shrimp or prawns from marinade; discard marinade. Cook shrimp or prawns and lobsters on grill until browned on both sides and just changed in color. Cook mussels on grill until shells have opened. Return scallops to shells, if desired; serve seafood with bread and lemon or lime wedges, if desired.

SERVES 6

Far left Blackened fish fillets with sweet tomato relish
Left Seafood brochettes with lime and coconut
Above Seafood platter

Above, from left Lemon and mustard calamari;
Tuna steaks with olive and feta salsa;
Right Chili lime snapper

LEMON AND MUSTARD CALAMARI

You will need to cook about 1⅓ cups raw white rice for this recipe. Some fish markets offer calamari (squid) hoods, which make preparation more convenient.

1½ tablespoons olive oil
**1 small white onion,
   chopped finely**
2 cloves garlic, crushed
4 green onions, chopped
4 cups cooked calrose rice
**½ cup coarsely grated
   parmesan cheese**
**1½ tablespoons finely grated
   lemon rind**
1 egg, beaten lightly
1½ tablespoons mild mustard
6 medium calamari hoods

⅓ cup olive oil
1 clove garlic, crushed
3 tablespoons lemon juice
2 teaspoons mild mustard
½ teaspoon sugar

Heat oil in pan; cook white onion and garlic, stirring, until onion is soft. Add green onion; cook, stirring, until just soft. Combine rice, onion mixture, cheese, rind, egg and mustard in large bowl. *[Can be made ahead to this stage. Cover, refrigerate overnight.]*

Spoon mixture into calamari hoods, securing ends with toothpicks. Cook calamari on heated oiled grill, uncovered, until browned all over and tender. Serve drizzled with Lemon and Mustard Dressing.

Lemon and Mustard Dressing Combine all ingredients in jar; shake well.

SERVES 4 TO 6

CHILI LIME SNAPPER

2 whole snapper
2 small hot red chilies,
    seeded, sliced
3 tablespoons grated lime rind
3 tablespoons chopped
    fresh cilantro
2 fresh kaffir lime leaves, shredded
1¹/₂ tablespoons sliced fresh
    lemon grass
1¹/₂ tablespoons grated fresh ginger
2 teaspoons Szechuan pepper
3 green onions, sliced thinly
1¹/₂ tablespoons fish sauce
1¹/₂ tablespoons lime juice
1¹/₂ tablespoons dark sesame oil

Cut fish 3 times on each side. Place each fish on a large piece of foil. Combine chili, rind, cilantro, lime leaves, lemon grass, ginger, pepper and onion in medium bowl; divide chili mixture between fish. Combine sauce, juice and oil; pour over fish. Seal foil to enclose fish. *[Best made ahead to this stage. Cover, refrigerate 3 hours or overnight.]*

Place fish on heated oiled grill. Cook, covered, using indirect heat, following manufacturer's instructions, 10 minutes. Carefully turn fish over; cook about 10 minutes or until just cooked through.

SERVES 4

TUNA STEAKS WITH OLIVE AND FETA SALSA

1¹/₂ tablespoons olive oil
1¹/₂ tablespoons lemon juice
1/₄ teaspoon cracked black pepper
8 tuna steaks

OLIVE AND FETA SALSA

4 medium tomatoes,
    seeded, chopped
1 cup pitted black olives, sliced
12oz feta cheese, chopped
1/₃ cup chopped
    fresh oregano
3 tablespoons pine nuts, toasted

Combine oil, juice and pepper in small bowl; brush over tuna. Cook tuna on heated oiled grill, uncovered, brushing occasionally with oil mixture, until browned on both sides and just cooked through. Serve immediately with Olive and Feta Salsa.

Olive and Feta Salsa Combine all ingredients in small bowl.

SERVES 8

Star skewers from Made on Earth

LOBSTER TAILS WITH AVOCADO AND BELL PEPPER

4 medium uncooked lobster tails
3 tablespoons butter, melted
2 cloves garlic, crushed

AVOCADO PUREE
2 medium avocados
1¹/₂ tablespoons lime juice

RED BELL PEPPER SAUCE
4 medium sweet red bell peppers
1¹/₂ tablespoons olive oil
1 medium white onion, chopped
1 clove garlic, crushed
¹/₂ cup chicken stock

Remove and discard skin from underneath lobster tails to expose flesh.

Cut each tail in half lengthwise. Combine butter and garlic in small bowl; brush over lobster flesh. Cook lobster on heated oiled grill, uncovered, until browned on both sides and changed in color. Serve lobster with Avocado Puree and Red Pepper Sauce.

Avocado Puree Blend or process the avocados and juice until nearly smooth.

Red Bell Pepper Sauce Quarter peppers; remove and discard seeds and membranes. Cook pepper, skin-side-down, on heated oiled grill until skin blisters and blackens. Cover pepper pieces in plastic or paper 5 minutes; peel away skin. Heat oil in small pan; cook onion and garlic, stirring, until onion is soft. Add pepper and stock; bring to boil. Remove from heat; blend or process pepper mixture until nearly smooth. *[Can be made a day ahead to this stage. Cover, refrigerate overnight.]*

SERVES 4

White oval plate from The Bay Tree

TUNA WITH CILANTRO PESTO

4 thick tuna steaks

CILANTRO PESTO

1/2 cup firmly packed fresh cilantro
1/4 cup peanut oil
**11/2 tablespoons unsalted
 roasted peanuts**
**1 small hot red chili,
 seeded, chopped**
3 tablespoons lime juice
2 teaspoons wasabi paste

Reserving half the Cilantro Pesto, brush tuna with remainder. Cook tuna on heated oiled grill, uncovered, until browned on both sides and just cooked through. Serve tuna with reserved Cilantro Pesto.

Cilantro Pesto Blend or process cilantro, oil, peanuts, chili, juice and paste until just smooth. *[Best made ahead to this stage. Cover, refrigerate for 3 hours or overnight.]*

SERVES 4

SMOKED TROUT WITH POTATO AND APPLE WEDGES

You need 8oz smoking chips for this recipe.

1 cup apple juice
3 tablespoons grated lemon rind
4 rainbow trout
1 medium white onion, sliced thinly
**3 tablespoons finely chopped
 fresh thyme**
11/2 tablespoons grated fresh ginger
**11/2 tablespoons grated lemon
 rind, extra**
1/3 cup olive oil
4 medium potatoes
2 teaspoons sea salt
4 medium apples
1 large pink grapefruit, sectioned
11/2 tablespoons sugar

Combine smoking chips, juice and rind in small bowl, stand 2 hours.

Cut 3 deep slits in each side of each fish. Combine onion, thyme, ginger, extra rind and half the oil; place a quarter of the onion mixture inside each cavity. Place fish in disposable baking dish. Place drained chips in smoke box; place on grill beside fish. Cook in covered grill, using indirect heat, following manufacturer's instructions, for about 30 minutes or until cooked through.

Meanwhile, peel potatoes, cut into wedges; place in disposable baking dish. Place potatoes on grill next to fish, sprinkle with salt, drizzle with remaining oil. Cook 20 minutes. Peel and core apples, cut into wedges. Place apple and grapefruit in dish with potato, sprinkle with sugar; cook 15 minutes or until potatoes and apples are tender.

SERVES 4

Left, from top Lobster tails with avocado and bell pepper; Tuna with cilantro pesto
Above Smoked trout with potato and apple wedges

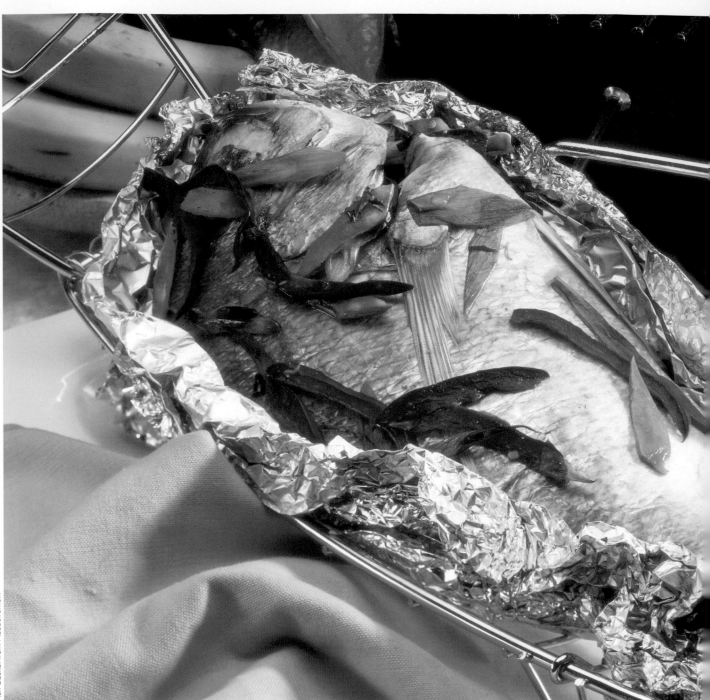

SNAPPER STUFFED WITH THAI-STYLE VEGETABLES

**2 medium sweet red bell peppers,
 sliced thinly**
6 green onions, sliced thinly
8oz snow peas, sliced thinly
**3 tablespoons thinly sliced
 fresh ginger**
3 tablespoons sweet chili sauce
2 teaspoons fish sauce
3 tablespoons lime juice
1/3 cup fresh basil
1/2 cup fresh cilantro
3lb whole snapper

Combine pepper, onion, snow peas, ginger, sauces, juice and herbs in medium bowl. Fill fish cavity with vegetable mixture. Wrap fish in oiled foil, place in fish grill, or on grill or grill plate. Cook in covered grill, using indirect heat, following manufacturer's instructions, about 45 minutes or until fish is just cooked through.

SERVES 4

TERIYAKI SNAPPER WITH SOBA

1/2 cup soy sauce
1/4 cup oyster sauce
3 tablespoons brown sugar
1/4 cup mirin
4 thick snapper steaks
8oz package soba noodles

Combine sauces, sugar and mirin in large bowl; add fish. *[Best made ahead to this stage. Cover, refrigerate for 3 hours or overnight.]*

Drain fish over small pan; reserve marinade. Cook fish on heated oiled grill,

COCO-LIME FISH WITH PAPAYA-RASPBERRY SALSA

3 tablespoons jaggery [see Glossary] or brown sugar
14oz can coconut milk
3 tablespoons finely grated kaffir lime rind
2 small hot red chilies, chopped finely
4 thick snapper steaks

PAPAYA-RASPBERRY SALSA

3 tablespoons raspberry vinegar
1/2 pint fresh raspberries
4 cups papaya, chopped
1 1/2 tablespoons chopped fresh mint

Combine sugar, milk, rind and chili in small pan. Simmer, stirring occasionally, for 10 minutes; cool. Pour coconut mixture over fish in large bowl. [*Best made ahead to this stage. Cover, refrigerate for 3 hours or overnight.*]

Drain fish over small pan; reserve marinade. Cook fish, uncovered, on heated oiled grill until browned on both sides and just cooked through. Meanwhile, place reserved marinade on grill, bring to boil; simmer, uncovered, until thickened slightly. Drizzle marinade over fish and serve with the Papaya-Raspberry Salsa.

Papaya-Raspberry Salsa Combine all ingredients in medium bowl; cover, refrigerate 30 minutes.

SERVES 4

uncovered, until browned on both sides and just cooked through.

Meanwhile, place reserved marinade on grill, bring to boil, simmer, uncovered, 2 minutes. Cook noodles according to directions on package; drain. Stir marinade through noodles. Serve fish on top of noodles.

SERVES 4

Right, from top Coco-lime fish with papaya-raspberry salsa; Teriyaki snapper with soba
Above Snapper stuffed with Thai-style vegetables

GINGER TUNA WITH WASABI DRIZZLE

1/2 cup olive oil
2 teaspoons grated fresh ginger
3 small hot red chilies, seeded, chopped finely
3 tablespoons chopped fresh lemon grass
4 thick tuna steaks

1 cup white wine
3 tablespoons jaggery [see Glossary] or brown sugar
1/3 cup cider vinegar
1 1/2 tablespoons wasabi paste
1 1/4 cup creme fraiche

Combine oil, ginger, chili and lemon grass in large bowl; add tuna. *[Best made ahead to this stage. Cover, refrigerate 3 hours or overnight.]*

Drain tuna over small bowl; reserve marinade. Cook tuna on heated oiled grill, uncovered, brushing with reserved marinade, until browned on both sides and just cooked through. Serve with Wasabi Drizzle.

Wasabi Drizzle Combine wine, sugar and vinegar in small pan; simmer, uncovered, until reduced by half, cool slightly. Stir in paste and creme fraiche. *[Can be made ahead. Cover, refrigerate overnight.]*

SERVES 4

ASIAN-STYLE SNAPPER IN BANANA LEAVES

If you can not find banana leaves at shops specializing in Asian foods, you can substitute four 12-inch squares aluminum foil.

4 large banana leaves
4 small bream or snapper
3 tablespoons grated fresh ginger
1/3 cup (about 1 stalk) thinly sliced fresh lemon grass
2 cloves garlic, crushed
1 1/2 tablespoons lime juice
3 tablespoons soy sauce
1/4 cup sweet chili sauce
1 teaspoon dark sesame oil
1 cup bean sprouts
8oz baby bok choy, chopped
2 trimmed stalks celery, sliced
4 green onions, chopped

Cut each banana leaf into 12-inch square. Using tongs, dip one leaf at a time into large pan of boiling water; remove immediately, rinse under cold water, dry leaves thoroughly. Leaves should be soft and pliable.

Cut fish 3 times on each side. Place each fish on a square of leaf; top with ginger and lemon grass. Combine garlic, juice, sauces and oil; drizzle a little mixture over each fish. Fold leaves over fish; secure packets with kitchen string. Place packets on grill, seam-side-down. Cook packets in covered grill, using indirect heat, following manufacturer's instructions, about 25 minutes or until just cooked through.

Combine sprouts, bok choy, celery and onion with remaining sauce mixture. Cook on heated oiled grill, until just cooked and tender. Serve vegetable mixture with fish.

SERVES 4

Left Ginger tuna with wasabi drizzle
Opposite Asian-style snapper in banana leaves

Fork from The Bay Tree

Above Salmon with watercress and dill pesto
Right Fish packets with cilantro salsa

SALMON WITH WATERCRESS AND DILL PESTO

1 (3lb) whole side salmon
1/2 cup mascarpone cheese

WATERCRESS AND DILL PESTO
**1/2 cup chopped
    fresh watercress**
1/2 cup chopped fresh dill
1/2 cup pine nuts, toasted
**2/3 cup coarsely grated
    parmesan cheese**
3 tablespoons grated lime rind
2 cloves garlic, crushed
1/3 cup olive oil

Remove skin and bones from salmon. Place salmon on large sheet of foil; spread with Watercress and Dill Pesto, wrap in foil. Cook salmon, pesto-side-up, on heated oiled grill, uncovered, 15 minutes. Open foil; cook about 5 minutes or until salmon is just cooked through. Discard foil; cut salmon into 4 pieces, top with mascarpone cheese.

Watercress and Dill Pesto Blend or process watercress, dill, nuts, cheese, rind and garlic until just chopped. With motor operating, gradually pour in oil; process until thick. *[Can be made ahead. Cover, refrigerate up to 1 week.]*

SERVES 4

FISH PACKETS WITH CILANTRO SALSA

You will need about 3 corn cobs with the husks intact for this recipe. Use small garfish, whiting or other small whole fish.

16 pieces corn husk
1 medium sweet red bell pepper
4 small whole fish
**1¹/₂ tablespoons finely grated
  lime rind**

CILANTRO SALSA
**2 medium tomatoes,
  seeded, chopped**
1 small red onion, chopped finely
1¹/₂ tablespoons lime juice
1¹/₂ tablespoons olive oil
**1¹/₂ tablespoons coarsely chopped
  fresh cilantro**

Cover husks with water in large bowl, cover, stand 3 hours or overnight; drain.
  Quarter pepper, remove seeds and membrane. Cook pepper, skin-side-down, on heated oiled grill until skin blisters and blackens. Cover pepper pieces in plastic or paper for 5 minutes, peel away skin, slice flesh. *[Can be made ahead. Cover, refrigerate overnight.]*

Using sharp scissors, cut backbone at tail end of each fish, flatten along backbone with rolling pin; gently peel out bone and discard.

Wrap fish in husks with pepper and rind; secure packets with kitchen string. Cook fish packets on heated oiled grill, uncovered, 5 minutes each side or until just cooked through. Serve with Cilantro Salsa.

Cilantro Salsa Combine all ingredients in small bowl.

SERVES 4

SARDINES IN CHERMOULLA WITH TOMATO SALSA

1/2 **cup firmly packed fresh Itallian parsley**
1/2 **cup firmly packed fresh cilantro**
4 **cloves garlic, crushed**
1 **medium red onion, chopped**
1 **teaspoon grated lemon rind**
1 **teaspoon ground cumin**
1 **teaspoon sweet paprika**
1 **teaspoon grated fresh ginger**
1/3 **cup peanut oil**
24 **fresh sardines, boned**
4 **medium tomatoes, seeded, chopped**

Blend or process parsley, cilantro, garlic, half the onion, rind, cumin, paprika, ginger and 1/4 cup of the oil until smooth. Reserve 2 tablespoons of the chermoulla. *[Best made ahead to this stage. Cover, refrigerate overnight.]*

Combine sardines with chermoulla in large bowl, cover; refrigerate 1 hour. Combine tomato, remaining onion, remaining oil and reserved chermoulla in small bowl. Cook sardines on heated oiled grill, uncovered, until sardines are browned on both sides and just cooked through; serve with tomato salsa.

SERVES 6

TUNISIAN PRAWNS WITH CILANTRO POTATOES

2lb **large uncooked prawns or jumbo shrimp**
1 **teaspoon ground cumin**
1 **teaspoon ground coriander**
1 **teaspoon hot paprika**
2 **cloves garlic, crushed**
2 **eggs, beaten lightly**
1 **cup shelled pistachios, toasted, chopped finely**

CILANTRO POTATOES

1 **cup firmly packed fresh cilantro**
1/3 **cup pine nuts**
1 **clove garlic, crushed**
3 **tablespoons lime juice**
1/4 **cup olive oil**
4 **large potatoes**

Shell and devein prawns, leaving tails intact. Place prawns in large shallow dish; add cumin, coriander, paprika and garlic, mix well. *[Best made ahead to this stage. Cover, refrigerate 3 hours or overnight.]*

Dip prawns in egg, coat in nuts; cook on heated oiled grill, uncovered, until browned on both sides and changed in color. Serve with Cilantro Potatoes.

Cilantro Potatoes Blend or process cilantro, pine nuts, garlic and juice until just smooth. With motor operating, gradually add oil. *[Best made ahead to this stage. Cover, refrigerate for 3 hours or overnight.]*

Slice potatoes, brush with cilantro mixture, place in disposable baking dish. Cook in covered grill, using indirect heat, following manufacturer's instructions, about 30 minutes or until potatoes are browned and tender.

SERVES 4

White bowls from The Bay Tree

SUGAR AND STAR-ANISE SMOKED SALMON

You need 12oz briquettes for this recipe. Sprinkled with sugar and spices, they lend a smoked flavor to the salmon.

2lb salmon fillet
1 cup gin
3 tablespoons brown sugar
2 teaspoons mixed spice
2/3 cup white sugar
3/4 cup star anise
1¹/2 tablespoons dill seeds

Combine salmon, gin, brown sugar and mixed spice in large bowl. *[Best made ahead to this stage. Cover, refrigerate for 3 hours or overnight.]*

   Place briquettes in disposable baking dish; light briquettes according to manufacturer's instructions. When flame has subsided and briquettes have a coating of ash, sprinkle with white sugar, star anise and dill seeds. Drain salmon; discard marinade. Place salmon on wire rack over briquettes; cover loosely with foil and cook in covered grill, using indirect heat, following manufacturer's instructions, about 20 minutes or until just cooked through.

SERVES 4 TO 6

Far left, from top Sardines in chermoulla with tomato salsa; Tunisian prawns with cilantro potatoes
Above Sugar and star-anise smoked salmon
Above right Lemon grass and chili-smoked swordfish

Glass plates and fork from Accoutrement; chair from The Edge Restaurant, Sydney

LEMON GRASS AND CHILI-SMOKED SWORDFISH

3lb piece swordfish
1¹/2 tablespoons grated fresh ginger
4 fresh small hot red chilies, chopped
1 cup olive oil
3 stalks fresh lemon grass, pounded
1/2 cup lemon grass tea
1 quart boiling water
1¹/2 tablespoons dried chili flakes

Cut swordfish into thick slices; combine with ginger, chili, oil and a quarter of the lemon grass in large shallow dish. *[Best made ahead to this stage. Cover, refrigerate for 3 hours or overnight.]*

   Combine tea, remaining lemon grass, water and chili in large disposable baking dish; place on grill. Drain swordfish over a bowl; reserve marinade. Place swordfish on wire rack over large baking dish. Cook in covered grill, using indirect heat, following manufacturer's instructions, 35 minutes or until just cooked through. Brush swordfish occasionally with reserved marinade.

SERVES 4 TO 6

Shell and devein prawns. Blend or process prawns, crab meat, chili and ginger until well combined. Using hands, shape 1/4 cup portions of mixture into patties. *[Best made ahead to this stage. Cover, refrigerate 3 hours, overnight or freeze.]*

Just before serving, toss patties in flour, shaking away excess. Cook, uncovered, on heated, oiled grill until patties are browned on both sides and cooked through. Serve with Sweet Chili Cucumber Salsa.

Sweet Chili Cucumber Salsa Combine all ingredients in small bowl.

MAKES 12

BUTTERFLIED HOT AND SOUR PRAWNS

2lb large uncooked prawns or jumbo shrimp
1/4 cup honey
1/4 cup light soy sauce
1 1/2 tablespoons hoi sin sauce
2 cloves garlic, crushed
1 small hot red chili, seeded, chopped
2 teaspoons sesame seeds

Shell and devein prawns, leaving tails intact. Cut along prawn backs, lengthwise, without separating halves. Combine honey, sauces, garlic and chili in medium bowl with prawns. *[Best made ahead to this stage. Cover, refrigerate for 3 hours or overnight.]*

Cook flattened prawns on heated oiled grill, uncovered, until browned on both sides and changed in color. Serve sprinkled with toasted sesame seeds.

SERVES 4

SALMON WITH DILL AND CAPER MAYONNAISE

6 salmon steaks
3 tablespoons lemon pepper seasoning
3 tablespoons drained capers

DILL AND CAPER MAYONNAISE
2 egg yolks
1 1/2 tablespoons lemon juice
2 teaspoons Dijon mustard
1/2 cup olive oil
1/2 cup vegetable oil
1 1/2 tablespoons drained capers, chopped
1 1/2 tablespoons chopped fresh dill
1 1/2 tablespoons grated lemon rind

Sprinkle salmon all over with seasoning; cook, uncovered, on heated oiled grill until browned on both sides and just cooked through. Cook capers on grill, uncovered, until well browned and crisp. Top salmon with capers and Dill and Caper Mayonnaise.

Dill and Caper Mayonnaise Blend or process egg yolks, juice and mustard until smooth. With motor operating, gradually

pour in combined oils; process until thick. Stir in capers, dill and rind. *[Can be made ahead. Cover, refrigerate up to 3 days.]*

SERVES 6

CRAB AND PRAWN CAKES WITH SALSA

1 1/2lb large uncooked prawns or jumbo shrimp
1lb shredded fresh crab meat
1 small hot red chili, seeded, chopped
1 teaspoon grated fresh ginger
all-purpose flour

SWEET CHILI CUCUMBER SALSA
4 small green cucumbers, seeded, chopped
1 medium sweet red bell pepper, seeded, chopped
1/4 cup sweet chili sauce
1 1/2 tablespoons fish sauce
1 1/2 tablespoons dry white wine
1 1/2 tablespoons brown sugar
3 tablespoons finely chopped fresh cilantro

Left Salmon with dill and caper mayonnaise
Right, from top Crab and prawn cakes with salsa; Butterflied hot and sour prawns

Pork

There's something special about pork sizzling on a grill. Crunchy crackling on a roast, simple pork sausages or a whole grilled ham – whatever your favorite, there's a recipe here to please you. Serve your pork dish with sweet potatoes roasted over the fire, or an accompaniment of grilled fresh seasonal fruit... and remember that leftover pork loin makes a great sandwich.

PORK CHOPS WITH PEPPER AND BRANDY CREAM SAUCE

- 1 small pear, peeled, sliced
- 2 tablespoons butter
- 1 medium onion, sliced
- 1 teaspoon brown sugar
- 1¹/₂ tablespoons water
- 6 thick pork chops

PEPPER AND BRANDY CREAM SAUCE

- ¹/₄ cup brandy
- 3 tablespoons drained pickled green peppercorns, crushed
- 1 cup cream
- 1¹/₂ tablespoons Worcestershire sauce

Cook pear on heated oiled grill until browned and tender. Melt butter in small pan on grill; cook onion, stirring, until browned lightly. Add pear, sugar and water; cook, stirring, until combined. Reserve a quarter of the pear mixture.

Cut small pocket in side of each chop; divide pear mixture among pockets, secure with toothpicks. Cook chops, uncovered, on heated oiled grill until browned on both sides and cooked as desired. Serve with Pepper and Brandy Cream Sauce.

Pepper and Brandy Cream Sauce Place reserved pear mixture in medium pan; add brandy, simmer until reduced by half. Add peppercorns, cream and sauce; cook, stirring, until sauce thickens slightly.

SERVES 6

SAUSAGES WITH TOFFEED APPLE AND SWEET-SOUR LEEK

- 2 large red apples
- ¹/₃ cup firmly packed brown sugar
- 4 tablespoons butter
- 2 large leeks, sliced
- 2 cloves garlic, crushed
- 3 tablespoons red wine vinegar
- 12 thick pork sausages

Core apples; cut each into 12 wedges. Combine apple with half of the sugar in small bowl. Heat butter in medium pan on grill; cook leek and garlic, stirring, until soft. Add vinegar and remaining sugar; cook, stirring, about 10 minutes or until leek is soft and caramelized.

Cook sausages, in batches, uncovered, on heated oiled grill until browned all over and cooked through. Cook apples on heated oiled grill until browned on both sides and just softened. Serve sweet-sour leek and toffeed apple with pork sausages.

SERVES 4 TO 6

From left Pork chops with pepper and brandy cream sauce; Pork sausages with toffeed apple and sweet-sour leek

Striped bowl from Orson & Blake

GINGER PORK WITH MANGO AND RED ONION SALSA

3 tablespoons grated fresh ginger
1¹/₂ tablespoons ground mustard
¹/₃ cup olive oil
4 pork butterfly steaks

MANGO AND RED ONION SALSA
2 medium red onions, sliced thinly
2 medium mangoes, sliced
3 tablespoons chopped
 fresh cilantro
¹/₄ cup raspberry vinegar
2 teaspoons sugar

Combine ginger, mustard and oil in large bowl; add pork, mix well. *[Best made ahead to this stage. Cover, refrigerate at least 3 hours or overnight.]*

Drain pork; discard marinade. Cook, uncovered, on heated oiled grill until browned on both sides and cooked as desired. Serve with Mango and Red Onion Salsa.

Mango and Red Onion Salsa Cook onion on heated oiled grill until browned and soft. Cook mango on heated oiled grill until browned all over. Combine onion and mango in medium bowl with remaining ingredients.

SERVES 4

MEDITERRANEAN PORK AND TAPENADE ROLL-UPS

²/₃ cup pitted black olives
¹/₄ cup olive oil
1 clove garlic, crushed
4 sun-dried tomatoes in oil,
 drained, chopped
1¹/₂ tablespoons chopped
 fresh oregano
1¹/₂ tablespoons balsamic vinegar
¹/₄ cup coarsely grated
 parmesan cheese
8 pork butterfly steaks
8 thin slices prosciutto

Blend or process olives, oil, garlic, tomato, oregano, vinegar and cheese until smooth. *[Can be made ahead to this stage. Cover, refrigerate overnight.]*

Place pork steaks between sheets of plastic wrap; pound with meat mallet until an even thickness. Divide olive paste into 8 equal portions; spread over surface of each steak, roll to enclose mixture. Wrap 1 slice of prosciutto around each roll; secure with toothpicks. Cook pork rolls, uncovered, on heated oiled grill, until browned all over and cooked as desired.

SERVES 8

ROAST LOIN OF PORK WITH CRACKLING AND APPLESAUCE

4lb boneless rolled loin of pork
3 tablespoons olive oil
3 tablespoons coarse cooking salt
6 medium apples
4 tablespoons butter, softened
1/4 cup firmly packed brown sugar
2 teaspoons ground cinnamon

Place pork in disposable baking dish; drizzle with some of the oil, rub salt into skin. Cook in covered grill, using indirect heat, following the manufacturer's instructions, 30 minutes. Brush with remaining oil; cook in covered grill about 45 minutes or until skin is browned and pork cooked as desired.

Meanwhile, peel, core and quarter apples. Divide among 4 sheets of foil; top with butter, sprinkle with sugar and cinnamon. Wrap foil to enclose apple mixture; place packets on grill alongside pork for final 15 minutes of pork cooking time. Blend or process apples until thick. Serve applesauce with pork.

SERVES 6 TO 8

PORK STEAKS WITH CARAWAY CABBAGE

4 pork loin medallion steaks
2 slices bacon, sliced thinly
1 medium onion, chopped finely
1 1/2 tablespoons caraway seeds
3 cups shredded cabbage
3 tablespoons brown sugar
1/4 cup cider vinegar
3 tablespoons butter
2 teaspoons finely chopped
** fresh sage**
3 tablespoons sour cream

Cook pork on heated oiled grill, un-covered, until browned on both sides and cooked through. Meanwhile, cook bacon, onion and seeds in medium pan until onion is soft. Add cabbage, cook, stirring, 2 minutes. Stir in sugar, vinegar and butter, cook, stirring, about 3 minutes or until cabbage is soft. Just before serving, stir in sage. Serve pork topped with cabbage and sour cream.

SERVES 4

Far left, from top Mediterranean pork and tapenade roll-ups; Ginger pork with mango and red onion salsa
Left Roast loin of pork with crackling and applesauce
Above Pork steaks with caraway cabbage

BBQ RIBS WITH BOSTON BAKED BEANS

1/2 cup barbecue sauce
1/4 cup tomato ketchup
3 tablespoons Worcestershire sauce
3 tablespoons mild chili sauce
3 tablespoons honey
2lb pork spareribs
2 cups great Northern beans
1 medium yellow onion, chopped
1 bay leaf
1/2 cup firmly packed brown sugar
1/4 cup mustard
1/2 cup molasses
2 cups water
1 teaspoon salt
7oz chopped bacon pieces

Combine sauces, ketchup and honey in large bowl, add ribs, mix well; cover, refrigerate overnight. Place beans in large bowl, cover with cold water; stand overnight.

Drain and rinse beans, place in large pan with onion and bay leaf. Cover bean mixture with cold water, bring to boil, simmer, uncovered, about 30 minutes or until beans are tender. Drain beans, discard bay leaf.

Place beans in disposable baking dish, stir in sugar, mustard, molasses, water and salt; sprinkle with bacon. Drain ribs over small bowl; reserve marinade. Place ribs in disposable baking dish. Cook ribs and beans in covered grill, using indirect heat, following the manufacturer's instructions, about 45 minutes or until ribs are tender and beans are slightly syrupy. During cooking, brush ribs occasionally with reserved marinade.

SERVES 4

CHILI PLUM RIBS AND SPICY POTATO WEDGES

1/2 cup plum sauce
3 tablespoons hot chili sauce
11/2 tablespoons tomato ketchup
11/2 tablespoons brown sugar
2lb pork ribs

SPICY POTATO WEDGES

11/2 tablespoons olive oil
1 teaspoon cajun seasoning
2 teaspoons garlic salt
6 medium potatoes

Combine sauces and sugar in small bowl; brush ribs with marinade. *[Best made ahead to this stage. Cover, refrigerate for 3 hours or overnight.]*

Place ribs in disposable baking dish; reserve any marinade in bowl. Cook ribs and Spicy Potato Wedges in covered grill, using indirect heat, following manu-

facturer's instructions, about 45 minutes or until cooked through. During cooking, brush the ribs occasionally with reserved marinade. Serve ribs with Spicy Potato Wedges.

Spicy Potato Wedges Combine oil, seasoning and garlic salt in large bowl. Cut each potato into 6 wedges; toss through oil mixture. Stand wedges skin-side-down in oiled disposable baking dish.

SERVES 4

TEX-MEX RIBS WITH CORN MUFFINS

1/2 cup barbecue sauce
1 teaspoon chili powder
21/2 tablespoons taco seasoning
2lb pork spareribs

CORN MUFFINS

11/2 tablespoons olive oil
1 small sweet red bell pepper, chopped
1 clove garlic, crushed
1/2 cup self-rising flour
1 cup cornmeal
1/2 teaspoon baking soda
5oz can corn kernels, drained
11/2 tablespoons chopped fresh cilantro
1/2 cup buttermilk
4 tablespoons butter, melted
1 egg, beaten lightly

Combine sauce, chili powder and seasoning in large bowl; add ribs, mix well. *[Best made ahead to this stage. Cover, refrigerate for 3 hours or overnight.]*

Place ribs in disposable baking dish. Cook in covered grill, using indirect heat, following manufacturer's instructions, 15 minutes. Place Corn Muffins next to ribs, continue to cook, covered, about 30 minutes or until ribs are tender and muffins cooked through. During cooking, brush ribs occasionally with pan juices. Serve with Corn Muffins.

Corn Muffins Heat oil in medium pan, add pepper and garlic; cook, stirring, until pepper is tender. Combine flour, cornmeal and soda in large bowl. Stir in pepper mixture, corn and cilantro, then stir in buttermilk, butter and egg. Divide mixture evenly among 4 greased muffin cups (1 cup capacity).

SERVES 4

Ribs, clockwise from center BBQ ribs with Boston baked beans; Chili plum ribs and spicy potato wedges; Tex-Mex ribs with corn muffins

ORANGE GLAZED HAM

12lb cooked leg of ham
2 small oranges, halved, sliced
whole cloves

ORANGE GLAZE

1/2 cup orange marmalade
3/4 cup orange juice
1/4 cup firmly packed
brown sugar
2 teaspoons Dijon mustard
3 tablespoons Cointreau or
Grand Marnier

Make a decorative cut through ham rind about 4-inches from the shank end of leg. Make a shallow cut down center of ham from one end to the other. Place ham on roasting rack or basket, or in disposable baking dish. Cook in covered grill, using indirect heat, following manufacturer's instructions, about 45 minutes or until skin begins to split. Remove from grill; cool 15 minutes. Peel skin away from ham carefully, leaving shank end intact; discard skin. Do not cut through surface of top fat or fat will spread during cooking. Secure orange slices with cloves in decorative pattern on ham. Wrap shank in foil; brush ham with Orange Glaze. Cook, covered, brushing occasionally with glaze, about 1 hour or until orange slices are lightly caramelized and ham is heated through.

Orange Glaze Mix all ingredients in small pan; stir over low heat until marmalade melts. *[Can be made ahead.]*

SERVES 12

THREE-PEPPER PORK

1 1/2 tablespoons black peppercorns
3 tablespoons green peppercorns
3 tablespoons ground lemon pepper
1/3 cup loosely packed fresh sage
3lb boneless pork loin
3 cups water

Process peppers and sage in spice grinder or blender until finely ground. Place pork, skin-side-down, on board; press pepper mixture over surface of meat. Roll from long side; tie with kitchen string at 1-inch intervals. *[Can be made ahead to this stage. Cover, refrigerate for 3 hours or overnight, or freeze.]*

Score pork skin; place in disposable baking dish with the water. Cook in covered grill, using indirect heat, following manufacturer's instructions, about 1 1/2 hours or until browned all over and cooked as desired.

SERVES 4 TO 6

PORK WITH ARTICHOKE AND SPINACH LOG

1/3 cup olive oil
1 clove garlic, crushed
3 tablespoons finely chopped
   fresh thyme
4 pork tenderloins
3 large potatoes, peeled, chopped
3 tablespoons butter
1 medium yellow onion,
   chopped finely
1 clove garlic, crushed, extra
2lb spinach, trimmed
14 1/2 oz can artichoke hearts,
   drained, chopped
2 cups water
2 cups dry red wine

Combine oil, garlic and thyme in large shallow dish; add pork, mix well. *[Best made ahead to this stage. Cover, refrigerate 3 hours or overnight.]*

Boil, steam or microwave potatoes until tender; drain, mash. Meanwhile, melt butter in medium pan; cook onion and extra garlic, stirring, until onion is soft. Place spinach in large heatproof bowl, cover with boiling water; drain, pat dry on absorbent paper. Combine potato and onion mixture in large bowl with artichoke hearts.

Place a piece of plastic wrap on counter; arrange spinach leaves in 8-inch x 12-inch rectangle on plastic wrap. Spoon artichoke mixture along center of spinach; fold one long side of spinach back over artichoke mixture to enclose it. Using plastic wrap as a guide, carefully roll to form log; twist ends tightly to hold shape. *[Best made ahead to this stage. Cover, refrigerate 3 hours or overnight.]*

Pour the water and wine into disposable baking dish. Drain pork; discard marinade. Place pork on wire rack over baking dish; cook in covered grill, using indirect heat, following manufacturer's instructions, about 30 minutes.

Meanwhile, remove plastic from artichoke and spinach log; wrap in foil, place on grill alongside pork for final 15 minutes of pork cooking time. Remove from grill when pork is cooked as desired and log heated through. Slice pork; cut log diagonally into 1 1/2-inch slices.

SERVES 4

Left Orange glazed ham
Right, from top Three-pepper pork;
Pork with artichoke and spinach log

Vegetables

Don't overcook your vegetables – they should retain a bit of crunch in the mouth while acquiring that subtle charred smokiness from the grill that makes this such a change from your everyday method of cooking them. These recipes make delicious meals in themselves, singly for lunch, or combined for a family meal. They also make great accompaniments, adding interest to meat dishes.

GARLIC CHILI POTATO KEBABS

Soak bamboo skewers in water about 1 hour to prevent them from scorching.

24 tiny new potatoes, unpeeled
12 baby onions
14 small hot red chilies
2 cloves garlic, crushed
3 tablespoons olive oil

Boil, steam or microwave potatoes and onions separately until just tender; drain. *[Can be made ahead to this stage. Cover, refrigerate overnight.]*
　Thread potatoes, onions and 12 of the chilies onto 4 skewers. Finely chop remaining chilies. Combine chili in small bowl with garlic and oil. Cook kebabs on heated oiled grill, brushing with chili mixture occasionally, until kebabs are browned all over and tender.

SERVES 4

CARROT AND DILL ROSTI

1/2 cup light sour cream
1 teaspoon ground cumin
11/2 tablespoons chopped fresh dill
5 medium carrots, grated
2 eggs, beaten lightly
1/3 cup all-purpose flour

Combine sour cream, cumin and dill in small bowl. *[Can be made a day ahead. Cover, refrigerate overnight.]*
　Combine carrot, eggs and flour in large bowl. Cook 1/4 cup portions of carrot mixture in batches on heated oiled grill plate, until rostis are browned both sides. Serve rostis with the sour cream mixture.

MAKES ABOUT 8

Right Garlic chili potato kebabs;
Carrot and dill rosti

BAKED RICOTTA WITH CHAR-GRILLED VEGETABLES

4 cups ricotta cheese
3 eggs, beaten lightly
3 tablespoons olive oil
1/2 teaspoon dried chili flakes

CHAR-GRILLED VEGETABLES
**1 large sweet red bell
    pepper, quartered**
**1 large sweet bell green
    pepper, quartered**
1 large eggplant, sliced
3 large zucchini, sliced
4 small plum tomatoes, quartered
2 medium lemons, quartered
3 small red onions, quartered
1/3 cup olive oil
**1 1/2 tablespoons cracked
    black pepper**

Combine ricotta with eggs in medium bowl; pour into greased 10-inch springform pan. Drizzle ricotta with oil, sprinkle with chili. Cover lightly with foil, cook in covered grill, using indirect heat, following manufacturer's instructions, for 15 minutes. Remove foil, cook for 10 minutes or until browned. Drain excess liquid from pan; cut ricotta into wedges. Serve with Char-grilled Vegetables.

Char-grilled Vegetables Combine all ingredients in large bowl. Cook vegetables on heated oiled grill, uncovered, until browned and tender.

SERVES 6 TO 8

CORN WITH SAGE AND BACON

4 corn cobs, unhusked
5 quarts water
1/4 cup milk
2 tablespoons chopped fresh sage
2 slices bacon, sliced thinly

Peel husks back from corn, leaving them attached at base; remove silk, fold husks back over corn. Soak corn in combined water and milk. *[Best made ahead. Cover, refrigerate for 3 hours or overnight.]*

Gently peel husk back from corn, press combined sage and bacon onto corn; tie husks with kitchen string to enclose filling. Place corn on grill rack. Cook in covered grill, using indirect heat, following manufacturer's instructions, about 40 minutes or until tender.

SERVES 4

Left Baked ricotta with char-grilled vegetables
Right, from top Corn with sage and bacon;
Potatoes with raclette cheese and garlic

POTATOES WITH RACLETTE CHEESE AND GARLIC

12 medium fingerling potatoes
1 bulb garlic
3 tablespoons butter
2 cups grated raclette or gruyere cheese

Wrap potatoes and whole garlic individually in foil. Place in disposable baking dish. Cook in covered grill, using indirect heat, following manufacturer's instructions, 30 minutes or until garlic is tender; remove garlic. Cook potatoes another 20 minutes or until tender. Cut garlic in half; squeeze out pulp into small bowl; stir in butter.

Partially unwrap potatoes; cut lengthwise down center, not cutting all the way through potato or foil. Open out potatoes, cup foil around them. Divide butter mixture among potatoes; top with cheese. Place in baking dish. Cook in covered grill, using indirect heat, following manufacturer's instructions, for 20 minutes or until cheese melts and bubbles.

SERVES 6

MUSTARD HONEY GLAZED VEGETABLES

1lb bunch baby carrots
1lb bunch baby beets
1lb bunch baby turnips
1lb bunch spring onions
3 tablespoons butter
¹⁄₄ cup honey

3 tablespoons stone ground mustard
1¹⁄₂ tablespoons lemon juice

Trim peeled carrots, beets, turnips and onions, leaving 1 inch of stems remaining. Combine remaining ingredients in small pan, stir over low heat until butter has melted. Combine vegetables in disposable baking dish with honey mixture. Cook in covered grill, using indirect heat, following manufacturer's instructions, for 40 minutes or until browned and tender.

SERVES 4 TO 6

Above Mustard honey glazed vegetables
Right, from top Mixed vegetables; Tomatoes with feta, olives and polenta

MIXED VEGETABLES

2 medium yellow zucchini
2 medium green zucchini
1 large sweet red bell pepper
1 large sweet yellow bell pepper
4 medium Japanese eggplants
4 spring onions
**7oz haloumi or fontina cheese,
    sliced thinly**
1 cup olive oil
**1¹/₂ tablespoons caraway seeds,
    toasted**
1¹/₂ tablespoons grated lemon rind
1 clove garlic, crushed
2 teaspoons ground cumin
**1¹/₂ tablespoons finely chopped
    fresh lemon thyme**
**3 tablespoons finely
    chopped capers**

Slice all vegetables thickly lengthwise. Cook vegetables and cheese on heated oiled grill, uncovered, until browned on both sides and tender. Transfer vegetables to large serving platter; drizzle with combined oil, seeds, rind, garlic, cumin, thyme and capers. Serve vegetables topped with cheese.

SERVES 6

TOMATOES WITH FETA, OLIVES AND CORNMEAL

3oz feta cheese, crumbled
1 clove garlic, crushed
1¹/₂ tablespoons olive oil
**1¹/₂ tablespoons finely chopped
    fresh lemon thyme**
4 large tomatoes
**²/₃ cup pitted black olives,
    sliced finely**
1¹/₂ tablespoons cornmeal

Combine cheese, garlic, oil and thyme in small bowl. *[Can be made ahead to this stage. Cover, refrigerate at least 3 hours or overnight.]*

Cut tomatoes in half horizontally; cut small slice from base so tomato halves sit flat. Cook, cut-side-down, on heated oiled grill until browned lightly. Transfer tomatoes, cut-side-up, to disposable baking dish. Top tomatoes with olives, feta mixture and cornmeal. Cook in covered grill, using indirect heat, following manufacturer's instructions, for 20 minutes or until browned.

SERVES 8

Dressed for success

A dressing adds its individual flavor to both salads and vegetables cooked on a grill. Here are a few classics, plus some of our favorites. At right, a chart that will make grilling vegetables a breeze.

HONEY DIJON DRESSING

1/4 cup honey
3 tablespoons Dijon mustard
1/2 cup white wine vinegar
11/2 tablespoons lemon juice
1 cup peanut oil

Combine honey, mustard, vinegar and juice in small bowl. Gradually whisk in oil; continue to whisk until dressing is slightly thickened and smooth.

MAKES ABOUT 2 CUPS

THOUSAND ISLAND DRESSING

1 cup mayonnaise
1/4 cup tomato paste
1/4 cup tomato ketchup
2 teaspoons Worcestershire sauce
1/2 teaspoon Tabasco sauce

Combine all ingredients in small bowl; whisk until smooth. Cover, refrigerate until needed.

MAKES ABOUT 11/2 CUPS

ROBBY'S DRESSING

2/3 cup extra virgin
   olive oil
2 shallots, chopped
3 tablespoons balsamic vinegar
3 tablespoons white vinegar
3 tablespoons lemon juice
2 teaspoons sugar
2 cloves garlic, crushed
2 teaspoons Dijon mustard

Blend or process all ingredients until thickened slightly and smooth.

MAKES ABOUT 11/2 CUPS

FRENCH DRESSING

1/2 cup olive oil
11/2 tablespoons white wine vinegar
2 teaspoons Dijon mustard
1/2 teaspoon sugar

Combine all ingredients in jar; shake well.

MAKES ABOUT 2/3 CUP

ITALIAN DRESSING

1/2 cup white vinegar
11/2 tablespoons lemon juice
1 teaspoon sugar
1/2 cup light olive oil
1 clove garlic, crushed
1/2 small white onion,
   chopped finely
1/2 small sweet red bell pepper,
   chopped finely
1/4 cup chopped fresh Italian
   parsley leaves

Combine all ingredients in jar; shake well.

MAKES ABOUT 11/2 CUPS

RUSSIAN DRESSING

1 cup mayonnaise
1/4 cup lemon juice
1/4 cup finely chopped gherkins
1 teaspoon sweet paprika
2 cloves garlic, crushed
11/2 tablespoons chopped fresh dill

Combine all ingredients in jar; shake well.

MAKES ABOUT 11/2 CUPS

CAESAR SALAD DRESSING

6 drained anchovy fillets
1 clove garlic, crushed
2 teaspoons Dijon mustard
2 teaspoons white vinegar
1 teaspoon sugar
1 egg yolk
1/2 cup vegetable oil
1/2 cup buttermilk

Blend or process anchovies, garlic, mustard, vinegar, sugar and egg yolk until combined. With motor operating, gradually add oil and buttermilk; process until thickened and smooth.

MAKES ABOUT 11/2 CUPS

VEGETABLE COOKING CHART

	Direct Heat	Indirect Heat
Artichokes	Boil, uncovered, 30 minutes, remove outer leaves, cut in half, remove hairy choke; grill until tender.	Boil, uncovered, 15 minutes, remove outer leaves and hairy choke, wrap in foil; grill until tender.
Asparagus	Brush or spray with oil; grill until tender.	
Baby bok choy	Cut in half lengthwise, brush or spray with oil; grill until tender.	Wrap whole baby bok choy in greased foil; grill until tender.
Beans (green, butter, long)	Wrap in foil with a little butter; grill until tender. Or, cook directly on grill plate until tender.	
Beets		Wrap whole unpeeled beet in foil; grill until tender then peel. Or, combine peeled, chopped beets with a little oil in a disposable baking dish; grill until tender.
Brussels sprouts	Cut in half, brush or spray with oil; grill until tender.	Wrap about 6 in foil with a little butter; grill until tender.
Carrots	Cut carrots in half lengthwise; boil, steam or microwave until almost tender; grill until tender.	Chop or slice carrots, combine with a little oil in a baking dish; grill until tender. Or, wrap whole baby carrots in foil; cook on warming rack until tender.
Corn	Soak unhusked corn in cold water overnight; grill in husks until tender. Or, grill thick slices of corn until tender.	Wrap in foil; grill until tender.
Eggplants	Cut into 1/2 inch slices, brush or spray with oil; grill until tender.	Prick whole eggplants all over with a skewer, grill in lightly oiled baking dish until tender; peel, chop flesh.
Fennel	Cut into slices; cook with a little butter on grill plate until tender.	Cut in half or slice, combine with a little oil in a baking dish; grill until tender.
Leeks	Cut in half lengthwise; grill until tender. Or, slice and cook on grill plate until tender.	Cut in half lengthwise or roughly chop, combine with a little oil in a baking dish; grill until tender.
Mushrooms	Brush or spray with oil; grill until tender.	Can be left whole or cut in half, combine mushrooms with a little oil in a baking dish; grill until tender.
Onions	Slice or chop; cook with a little oil on grill plate. Or, cut unpeeled onions in half; grill on grill plate until tender.	Peel and wrap whole onions in foil; grill until tender. Or, can be chopped or sliced and combined with a little oil in a baking dish; grill until tender.
Parsnips, turnips		Chop or slice, combine with a little oil in a baking dish; grill until tender.
Bell Peppers	Quarter peppers, remove seeds and membranes; grill, skin-side-down, until tender.	Place whole or filled peppers in baking dish; grill until tender. Or, wrap in foil; grill until tender.
Potato, sweet	Cut into thin slices, brush or spray with oil; grill until tender.	Grill whole wrapped in foil until tender. Or, can be chopped or sliced and combined with a little oil in a baking dish; grill until tender.
Rutabaga	Cut into thin slices, brush or spray with oil; grill until tender.	Wrap whole in foil; grill until tender. Or, can be chopped or sliced and combined with a little oil in a baking dish; grill until tender.
Squash, winter	Cut unpeeled squash or pumpkin into thin slices, brush or spray with oil; grill until tender.	Chop or slice squash, combine with a little oil in a baking dish; grill until tender. Small varieties can be wrapped in foil; grill until tender.
Tomatoes	Cut in half, brush or spray with oil; grill until tender.	Cut tomatoes in half, combine with a little oil in a baking dish; grill until tender.
Zucchini	Cut unpeeled zucchini in halves lengthwise, brush or spray with oil; grill until tender	Chop or slice, combine with a little oil in a baking dish; grill until tender. Or, wrap whole zucchini in foil; cook on warming rack until tender.

Breads and Desserts

Desserts and breads aren't the first things that come to mind when we think of grilling. But it's surprising how well they take to this method of cooking. Fruits, in particular, develop a deeper, richer flavor when grilled, while "baking" in a covered grill is similar to using old-fashioned, wood-fired ovens. This creates crusty breads and lends them a lovely, smoky character.

CHAR-GRILLED FRUITS

You will need about 3 passion fruit for this recipe. Star fruit (carambola) is most abundant at produce markets from August to February

- 1/2 **medium pineapple**
- 2 **star fruit (carambolas)**
- 2 **small bananas**
- 2 **medium mangoes**
- 2/3 **cup coconut-rum liqueur**
- 1/4 **cup passion fruit pulp**
- 1 1/2 **tablespoons brown sugar**
- 2 **cups cream, whipped**
- 3 **tablespoons flaked coconut, toasted**

Remove and discard top and base from pineapple; cut pineapple into 1/2 inch-thick slices, cut each slice in half. Cut star fruit into 1/2 inch slices. Slice bananas in half lengthwise. Cut mangoes down each side of seeds; cut a criss-cross pattern into flesh.

Combine liqueur, 2 tablespoons of the passion fruit pulp and sugar in medium pan. Stir over low heat, without boiling, until sugar dissolves. Bring to boil; simmer, uncovered, 5 minutes. Reserve 3 tablespoons of the passion fruit syrup. Combine fruit with remaining passion fruit syrup in large bowl. Cook fruit, in batches, on heated oiled grill, brushing occasionally with syrup, until browned on both sides and tender. Combine reserved passion fruit syrup with remaining passion fruit pulp in small bowl. Drizzle warm fruit with passion fruit syrup. Serve fruit with cream sprinkled with coconut.

SERVES 6 TO 8

Jig from Shack; green tumbler from Empire Homewares; blue plate and pearl spoon from The Bay Tree Kitchen Shop; barbecue from Kangaroo Tent-City & BBQ's

DAMPER

Damper is a rustic quick bread made from a butter-rich scone-like dough.

3 cups self-rising flour
1 teaspoon salt
7 tablespoons butter
1/2 cup milk
1/2 cup water, approximately

Combine flour and salt in bowl; rub in butter. Pour in milk and enough water to mix to a soft, sticky dough. Turn dough onto floured surface; knead lightly. Knead dough into a round shape, place in disposable baking dish. Press dough into a 6-inch round. Using a sharp knife, cut a cross in top of dough about 1/2-inch deep. Brush top of dough with a little extra milk, sift a little extra flour over top. Cook in covered grill, using indirect heat, following manufacturer's instructions, about 35 minutes or until damper sounds hollow when tapped.

SERVES 6 TO 8

PUMPKIN AND WALNUT DAMPER

You will need to cook about 1 2/3 cups chopped raw pumpkin for this recipe.

3 cups self-rising flour
4 tablespoons butter
1 cup chopped walnuts
1 1/2 cups cooked mashed pumpkin
1/2 cup buttermilk, approximately

Grease 8-inch round layer cake pan. Place flour in medium bowl; rub in butter, stir in nuts, pumpkin and enough buttermilk to mix to a soft, sticky dough. Turn dough onto floured surface, knead until smooth. Place into prepared pan. Cook in covered grill, using indirect heat, following manufacturer's instructions, about 30 minutes or until damper sounds hollow when tapped.

SERVES 4 TO 6

BOSTON BROWN BREAD

1 cup cornmeal
1 cup rye flour
1 cup whole-wheat flour
2 teaspoons baking soda
1 teaspoon salt
2 cups buttermilk
3/4 cup molasses
1 cup raisins

Combine cornmeal, flours, soda and salt in medium bowl; stir in buttermilk, molasses and raisins. Spoon mixture into greased 5 1/2 x 8 1/2-inch loaf pan. Cover top of pan with greased baking paper; cover tightly with a sheet of foil. Stand pan in disposable baking dish, pour in enough boiling water to come halfway up sides of pan; cover baking dish with foil. Cook in covered grill, using indirect heat, following manufacturer's instructions, about 2 hours or until bread is done when tested. Let bread stand in pan for 5 minutes before turning onto wire rack to cool.

SERVES 4 TO 6

MIXED SEED BEER BREAD

3 1/4 cups self-rising flour
2 teaspoons salt
2 teaspoons sugar
1/2 cup sunflower seed kernels
3 tablespoons poppy seeds
1/2 cup sesame seeds
1/2 cup flax seeds
1 1/2 cups beer

Combine flour, salt and sugar in medium bowl, stir in seeds; pour in beer all at once. Using spoon, mix to a soft, sticky dough. Knead on a floured surface until smooth. Shape into a 4 1/2 x 16-inch rectangle, place in oiled disposable baking dish or on oiled foil. Using a sharp knife, make 3 shallow cuts across top of dough. Cook in covered grill, using indirect heat, following manufacturer's instructions about 1 hour or until bread is browned and sounds hollow when tapped.

SERVES 6 TO 8

Above, from left Mixed seed beer bread; Boston brown bread
Right, from top Damper; Pumpkin and walnut damper; Peppered spinach and feta damper

PEPPERED SPINACH AND FETA DAMPER

3¹/₂ cups self-rising flour
1 teaspoon salt
2 teaspoons cracked black pepper
1¹/₂ tablespoons sugar
3 tablespoons butter
1 cup feta cheese, crumbled
3 cups baby spinach leaves, chopped

¹/₂ cup buttermilk
1 cup water, approximately

Combine flour, salt, pepper and sugar in large bowl; rub in butter. Stir in cheese, spinach, buttermilk and enough water to make a soft, sticky dough. Turn dough onto floured surface, knead until just smooth. Divide dough in half, place in greased disposable baking dish, press each half into a 4 inch round. Cut a cross in dough, about ¹/₂-inch deep. Brush with a little extra buttermilk, then sift a little extra flour over dough. Cook in covered grill, using indirect heat, following manufacturer's instructions, about 40 minutes or until cooked.

SERVES 6 TO 8

PEARS WITH RICOTTA, DATE AND MAPLE FILLING

1¹/4 cups ricotta cheese
¹/4 cup chopped pitted dates
¹/4 teaspoon ground cinnamon
1 teaspoon sugar
4 medium pears
¹/2 cup maple syrup
¹/4 cup water

Combine cheese, dates, cinnamon and sugar in small bowl. *[Can be made ahead to this stage. Cover, refrigerate overnight.]*

Cut pears in half lengthwise; using a teaspoon, scoop out seeds. Place a heaped tablespoon of cheese mixture in hollow of each pear half. Place pears in disposable baking dish, drizzle with combined maple syrup and water. Cover tightly with greased foil, cook in covered grill, using indirect heat, following manufacturer's instructions, 30 minutes or until pears are tender.

SERVES 8

MAPLE APPLES WITH ALMONDS AND MASCARPONE

4 large apples
¹/2 cup maple syrup
¹/2 cup flaked almonds
¹/4 teaspoon ground cinnamon
2 teaspoons confectioners' sugar
³/4 cup mascarpone cheese

Peel and core apples. Place in small disposable baking dish; pour maple syrup over apples. Cook in covered grill, using indirect heat, following the

SUGARED BRIOCHE SURRISES

1 cup pitted prunes, halved
1/3 cup brandy
4 sugared brioche
3/4 cup chopped hazelnuts, toasted
3 1/2 oz dark chocolate,
** chopped roughly**
3 tablespoons superfine sugar
3 eggs, beaten lightly

Place prunes and brandy in medium bowl. *[Best made ahead to this stage. Cover, refrigerate 3 hours or overnight.]*

Slice top off each brioche; carefully scoop out and reserve inside crumbs, leaving a thin shell. Blend or process reserved crumb until mixture resembles fine breadcrumbs. Combine crumbs and prune mixture in medium bowl with remaining ingredients. Divide prune mixture among brioche; replace tops. Place brioche on wire cake rack in disposable baking dish; cover lightly with foil. Cook in covered grill, using indirect heat, following the manufacturer's instructions, 10 minutes. Remove foil, cook 2 minutes or until tops are crisp.

MAKES 4

Left, from top Maple apples with almonds and mascarpone; Pears with ricotta, date and maple filling
Below Sugared brioche surprises

manufacturer's instructions, 10 minutes. Turn apples, brush with maple syrup from dish, cook 15 minutes or until tender.

Meanwhile, place almonds on small oven tray, sprinkle with combined cinnamon and icing sugar. Cook in covered grill 5 minutes or until almonds are toasted.

Serve apples drizzled with syrup from dish, topped with mascarpone and scattered with almonds.

SERVES 4

Sweet pizzas

We used frozen plain pizza crusts for these recipes. To make your own, use a third of the quantity of the basic dough recipe on page 106.

STRAWBERRY PIZZA WITH MASCARPONE

10-inch pizza crust
1/4 cup strawberry jam
1 1/2 tablespoons Cointreau
1 pint strawberries, halved
1/2 cup mascarpone cheese
2 teaspoons Cointreau, extra
2 teaspoons confectioners' sugar

Cook pizza crust on heated oiled grill until browned on both sides. Spread with combined jam, liqueur and strawberries. Cook in covered grill, using indirect heat, following manufacturer's instructions, about 10 minutes or until crust is crisp. Serve topped with combined cheese, extra liqueur and icing sugar.

SERVES 4

BAKED FIG AND DATE RICOTTA PIZZA

10-inch pizza crust
1 egg yolk
1 1/4 cups ricotta cheese
1/2 cup finely chopped, pitted dates
4 medium figs, sliced thinly
1 1/2 tablespoons brown sugar

Cook pizza crust on heated oiled grill until browned on both sides. Combine egg yolk and cheese in small bowl; stir in dates. Spread mixture over pizza crust. Arrange figs over cheese mixture. Sprinkle figs with sugar. Cook pizza in covered grill, using indirect heat, following the manufacturer's instructions, about 10 minutes or until figs are tender.

SERVES 4

CARDAMOM SPICED APPLE PIZZA

10-inch pizza crust
4 large apples, peeled, cored
10 cardamom pods
1/4 cup water
1 1/2 tablespoons butter
1 1/2 tablespoons superfine sugar
2 1/2 oz cream cheese, softened
1 1/2 tablespoons cream
2 teaspoons brown sugar
1 vanilla bean
1 1/2 tablespoons confectioners' sugar

Cook pizza crust on heated oiled grill until browned on both sides. Roughly chop 3 of the apples. Wrap cardamom in cheesecloth. Combine chopped apple, water, butter, cardamom and superfine sugar in medium pan. Simmer apple mixture, stirring, until apple is soft and pulpy; discard cardamom pods.

Meanwhile, combine cream cheese, cream, brown sugar and the seeds scraped from the vanilla bean in small bowl. Spread mixture over prepared pizza crust; top with apple mixture. Thinly slice remaining apple, arrange overlapping slices on apple mixture; sprinkle with confectioners' sugar. Cook pizza in covered grill, using indirect heat, following manufacturer's instructions, about 10 minutes or until apple slices are tender.

SERVES 4

CARAMEL BANANA PIZZA

10-inch pizza crust
2 small bananas, sliced

CARAMEL SAUCE
2/3 cup cream
1/4 cup firmly packed brown sugar
1 1/2 tablespoons maple syrup
1 tablespoon butter

Cook pizza crust on heated oiled grill until browned on both sides. Top with Caramel Sauce and banana. Cook in covered grill, using manufacturer's instructions about 10 minutes or until bananas are soft and crust is crisp.

Caramel Sauce Combine all ingredients in small pan; cook over low heat, without boiling, until sugar dissolves. Bring to boil, simmer, uncovered, until thickened.

SERVES 4

Below, from left Strawberry pizza with mascarpone; Baked fig and date ricotta pizza; Cardamom spiced apple pizza; Caramel banana pizza

RHUBARB GINGER SAUCE

3 cups chopped rhubarb
¹/₂ cup superfine sugar
1¹/₂ tablespoons chopped
candied ginger

Combine rhubarb and sugar in medium pan, stir over heat, without boiling, until sugar dissolves. Bring to boil, simmer, uncovered, about 8 minutes or until rhubarb is very soft. Blend or process mixture with ginger until smooth. Serve over ice-cream.

MAKES ABOUT 1 CUP

CARAMEL PISTACHIO SAUCE

1¹/₂ cups heavy cream
1 tablespoon butter
¹/₄ cup honey
¹/₂ cup firmly packed brown sugar
¹/₃ cup roughly chopped shelled
pistachios, toasted

Combine cream, butter, honey and sugar in medium pan. Bring to boil, stirring; simmer, uncovered, about 10 minutes or until sauce thickens slightly. Stir in nuts. Serve warm or cold over ice-cream.

MAKES ABOUT 2 CUPS

SUMMER BERRY COMPOTE

1 pint fresh blueberries
¹/₂ pint fresh raspberries
¹/₂ pint fresh blackberries
¹/₂ cup confectioners' sugar

Combine berries in large bowl. Place half the berries and sugar in medium pan over low heat. Cook, uncovered, about 5 minutes or until berries have softened. Blend or process berry mixture until smooth. Stir in remaining berries. Cover; refrigerate 1 hour before serving with cream, yogurt or ice-cream.

MAKES ABOUT 3 CUPS

PINEAPPLE COCONUT SAUCE

14oz can crushed pineapple, drained
¹/₄ cup coconut-rum liqueur
1¹/₂ cups cream
¹/₂ cup coconut milk

Blend or process pineapple, liqueur, cream and coconut milk until almost smooth. Serve sauce over ice-cream with toasted flaked coconut, if desired.

MAKES ABOUT 4 CUPS

Above, from left Rocky road sauce; Pineapple coconut sauce; Rhubarb ginger sauce; Summer berry compote; Caramel pistachio sauce; Lemon and passion fruit syrup

ROCKY ROAD SAUCE

1¹/₂ cups heavy cream
3¹/₂ oz dark chocolate, chopped
¹/₂ cup marshmallows
3 tablespoons chopped unsalted
roasted peanuts

Combine cream and chocolate in small pan, stir over low heat until chocolate has melted. Add marshmallows and peanuts, stir over low heat until marshmallows have almost melted. Serve warm or cold over ice-cream.

MAKES ABOUT 2 CUPS

LEMON AND PASSION FRUIT SYRUP

³/₄ cup water
¹/₄ cup lemon juice
³/₄ cup superfine sugar
¹/₃ cup fresh passion fruit pulp

Combine water, juice and sugar in small pan. Stir over heat, without boiling, until sugar is dissolved. Add passion fruit, bring to boil, simmer, uncovered, until syrup thickens slightly. Serve syrup with ice-cream.

MAKES ABOUT 1 CUP

FIGS, HONEYCOMB AND CINNAMON ICE-CREAM

Fresh honeycomb is available from natural food stores.

6 medium figs
1lb fresh honeycomb
1 pint vanilla ice-cream
2 teaspoons ground cinnamon

Cut figs in half lengthwise. Cook on heated oiled grill until browned. Cut honeycomb into 3/4-inch strips. Combine ice-cream and cinnamon. Serve figs with honeycomb and cinnamon ice-cream.

SERVES 4 TO 6

CARAMELIZED PEACHES WITH SPICED YOGURT

6 medium peaches, peeled, halved
1/4 cup firmly packed brown sugar

SPICED YOGURT
1 cup yogurt
1/4 teaspoon ground cinnamon
1/4 teaspoon ground cardamom

Cook prepared peaches on heated oiled grill griddle plate until browned; sprinkle with sugar, cook, turning, until sugar dissolves and starts to bubble. Serve with Spiced Yogurt.

Spiced Yogurt Combine all ingredients in small bowl.

SERVES 4

ARUGULA PESTO AND PARMESAN TURKISH BREAD

Turkish bread is a flat, oblong or round loaf topped with sesame seeds.

1/4 cup pine nuts, toasted
1 1/2 oz arugula
1 clove garlic, crushed
1/4 cup finely grated
 parmesan cheese
1/4 cup light olive oil
3 1/2 oz parmesan cheese, extra
16-inch long Turkish bread

Blend or process pine nuts, arugula, garlic and grated cheese until almost smooth. With motor operating gradually pour in oil. *[Can be made ahead to this stage. Cover, refrigerate overnight.]*

Using a vegetable peeler shave extra cheese into thin strips.

Place bread on oven tray, spread top with pesto, sprinkle with shaved cheese. Cook in covered grill, using indirect heat, following manufacturer's instructions, about 10 minutes or until cheese melts and is browned lightly.

SERVES 4

OLIVE TAPENADE AND MOZZARELLA TURKISH BREAD

2/3 cup pitted black olives
3 tablespoons coarsely chopped
 fresh parsley
2 teaspoons grated lemon rind
1 1/2 tablespoons lemon juice
1 clove garlic, crushed
3 tablespoons drained capers
16-inch long Turkish bread
8oz mozzarella cheese,
 sliced thinly

Blend or process olives, parsley, rind, juice, garlic and capers until almost smooth. *[Can be made ahead. Cover, refrigerate overnight.]*

Place bread on oven tray, spread top with olive tapenade, top with cheese. Cook in covered grill, using indirect heat, following manufacturer's instructions, about 10 minutes or until cheese melts and is browned lightly.

SERVES 4

Left, from top Figs, honeycomb and cinnamon ice-cream; Caramelized peaches with spiced yogurt
Right, clockwise from top left Arugula pesto and parmesan Turkish bread; Olive tapenade and mozzarella Turkish bread; Turkish bread with sun-dried tomato butter; Turkish bread with garlic and chive butter

TURKISH BREAD WITH SUN-DRIED TOMATO BUTTER

8 tablespoons butter, softened
3 tablespoons finely chopped
 drained sun-dried tomatoes
1 1/2 tablespoons finely
 chopped fresh basil
2 6-inch rounds Turkish bread

Combine butter, tomato and basil in small bowl. *[Can be made ahead. Cover, refrigerate overnight.]*

Split Turkish bread in half, cut each half into 3 pieces. Cook bread on heated oiled grill until browned on both sides. Spread with sun-dried tomato butter.

SERVES 4

TURKISH BREAD WITH GARLIC AND CHIVE BUTTER

4 cloves garlic
8 tablespoons butter, softened
1 1/2 tablespoons finely chopped
 fresh chives
2 6-inch rounds Turkish bread

Place unpeeled garlic in dry heavy-bottomed pan, cook over low heat until browned all over; remove skin.

Combine butter, chives and finely chopped garlic in small bowl. *[Can be made ahead. Cover, refrigerate overnight.]*

Split Turkish bread in half. Cut each half into 3 pieces. Cook bread on heated oiled grill until browned on both sides. Spread with garlic and chive butter.

SERVES 4

Wooden tray from Corso de' Fiori

DATE DUMPLINGS IN BUTTERSCOTCH SAUCE

1/3 cup chopped pitted dates
3 tablespoons boiling water
1 1/4 cups self-rising flour
2 tablespoons butter, chopped
1/2 cup milk,
approximately

BUTTERSCOTCH SAUCE
3/4 cup firmly packed
brown sugar
10 tablespoons butter, chopped
3/4 cup cream

Combine dates and the water in small bowl; stand 10 minutes or until dates are soft. Place flour in medium bowl; rub in butter. Add undrained date mixture and enough milk to mix to a soft, sticky dough. Pour hot Butterscotch Sauce into 10-cup capacity ovenproof dish or 10 1/2 x 14-inch disposable baking dish. Drop tablespoons of dumpling mixture into sauce. Cover dish, cook in covered grill, using indirect heat, following manufacturer's instructions, 15 minutes or until dumplings are firm.

Butterscotch Sauce Combine all ingredients in medium pan; stir over heat, without boiling, until sugar dissolves. Simmer, without stirring, 3 minutes.

SERVES 4 TO 6

RASPBERRY PECAN BREAD-AND-BUTTER PUDDING

10 slices raisin bread
3 tablespoons butter, softened
1/2 pint raspberries
3 eggs
1/4 cup superfine sugar
2 1/2 cups milk
1 teaspoon vanilla extract
1/2 cup chopped pecans
3 tablespoons brown sugar
3 tablespoons honey

Trim crusts from bread, spread both sides of bread with butter, cut each slice into 4 triangles. Arrange the bread in two 5 x 7-inch (4-cup capacity) ovenproof dishes or disposable baking dishes, sprinkle with raspberries. Whisk eggs, superfine sugar, milk and extract in large bowl; pour over bread. Sprinkle with combined nuts and brown sugar. Cook puddings in covered grill, using indirect heat, following the manufacturer's instructions, 45 minutes or until custard has set. Serve drizzled with honey.

SERVES 4

BASIC PIZZA DOUGH

Each of the following toppings is enough for one recipe of this Basic Pizza Dough. Cook crust in covered grill, using indirect heat, following manufacturer's instructions, 5 minutes, then turn dough over before covering with topping. There are also many ready-made pizza crusts on the market.

1 1/2 teaspoons (1/4 oz package)
yeast
1 cup warm water
2 teaspoons sugar
3 cups all-purpose flour
1 teaspoon salt

Whisk yeast, water and sugar in small bowl; cover, let stand in warm place about 10 minutes or until mixture is frothy. Sift flour and salt into large bowl, stir in yeast mixture; mix to a soft dough. Knead dough on floured surface about 10 minutes or until smooth. Place dough in large oiled bowl; cover, let stand in warm place about 1 hour or until dough is doubled in size.

To make mini pizzas, divide dough into 8 portions, roll each portion into a 6-inch round. To make plate-size pizzas, divide dough into 4 portions, roll each portion into a 10-inch round. Cook dough on rack, in covered grill, using indirect heat, following manufacturer's instructions, 5 minutes (dough may puff up; if it does, flatten, allowing air to escape). Turn dough over. Cover with any of the following toppings.

SERVES 4 TO 8

CHORIZO PIZZA

1/3 cup bottled pasta sauce
1lb chorizo sausage, sliced
1 medium white onion, sliced
1 medium sweet red bell
   pepper, sliced
1/2 cup pitted black olives, sliced
3 tablespoons chopped
   fresh basil
8oz bocconcini or mozzarella
   cheese, sliced

Spread cooked pizza crust with sauce, top with sausage, onion, pepper, olives, basil and cheese. Cook in covered grill, using indirect heat, following manufacturer's instructions, about 10 minutes or until cheese has melted.

ROASTED VEGETABLE PIZZA

4 Japanese eggplants, sliced
3 medium zucchini, sliced
1/2 cup sun-dried tomato pesto
1 medium sweet red bell pepper,
   seeded, chopped
7oz haloumi or fontina
   cheese, sliced

Cook eggplant and zucchini on heated oiled grill until just tender. Spread cooked pizza crust with pesto, top with eggplant, zucchini, pepper and cheese. Cook in covered grill, using indirect heat, following manufacturer's instructions, about 10 minutes or until cheese has melted.

THREE-MUSHROOM PIZZA

1 1/2 tablespoons butter, melted
1 clove garlic, crushed
4oz button mushrooms, sliced
4oz brown mushrooms, sliced
4oz oyster mushrooms, halved
1/2 cup coarsely grated smoked
   cheddar cheese
1/2 cup finely grated
   parmesan cheese
1 cup coarsely grated cheddar cheese

Brush cooked pizza crust with combined butter and garlic, top with mushrooms and cheese. Cook in covered grill, using indirect heat, following manufacturer's instructions, about 10 minutes or until cheese has melted.

SATAY SHRIMP PIZZA

1/2 cup bottled satay marinade
1 medium yellow onion, sliced
4oz snow peas, sliced thinly
8oz small uncooked shrimp or
   prawns, shelled
1/2 cup roasted cashews
3 tablespoons chopped
   fresh cilantro
1 cup coarsely grated
   mozzarella cheese

Spread cooked pizza crust with satay marinade, top with onion, snow peas, prawns or shrimp, cashews, cilantro and cheese. Cook in covered grill, using indirect heat, following manufacturer's instructions, about 10 minutes or until cheese has melted.

Left, from top Date dumplings in butterscotch sauce; Raspberry pecan bread-and-butter pudding
Above, clockwise from top left Chorizo pizza; Three-mushroom pizza; Roasted vegetable pizza; Satay shrimp pizza

Menu suggestions

Although many cook-outs are spontaneous events, a little planning can result in a superlative meal. Choose salads and other accompaniments according to your preferences and the season. The number of servings in each recipe may vary, so please adjust quantities to cover the numbers you're feeding.

FUSION CUISINE

Balsamic-flavored octopus

Tomato and mozzarella lamb stacks

Pumpkin and walnut damper

Maple apples with almonds and mascarpone

A day ahead: Clean and marinate octopus; toast almonds for maple apples.

3 hours ahead: Cook and mash pumpkin for damper.

OH CALCUTTA!

Indian spiced beef with dal

Tandoori chicken with cucumber mint raita

Indian chutney

Fresh fruit

Up to 1 week ahead: Make Indian chutney.

A day ahead: Prepare Indian spiced beef; marinate chicken in tandoori mixture.

3 hours ahead: Make cucumber and mint raita; soak smoking chips in wine.

1 hour ahead: Make dal.

THE SPICE IS RIGHT

Tuna with cilantro pesto

Indian spiced lamb with potato cakes

Spiced yogurt

A day ahead: Marinate lamb; make cilantro pesto.

3 hours ahead: Prepare both potato and yogurt mixtures.

IMPRESSING THE IN-LAWS

Crab and prawn cakes with sweet chili cucumber salsa

Chicken with caramelized pear

Baby bok choy with red onion and balsamic jam

Char-grilled fruits

A day ahead: Make crab and prawn cakes (or make ahead and freeze); slice and flatten chicken, refrigerate between layers of plastic wrap; make red onion and balsamic jam.

3 hours ahead: Make sweet chili cucumber salsa; prepare fruits for grilling; make passion fruit syrup.

AN AEGEAN MEDLEY

Lemon and mustard calamari

Greek-style beef with tzatziki and salad

Baked fig and date ricotta pizza

A day ahead: Make calamari seasoning mixture and its lemon and mustard dressing; marinate beef and make dressing for its salad.

3 hours ahead: Fill calamari hoods with seasoning; make tzatziki; prepare ricotta mixture for pizza.

LIGHT AND LOVELY

Grilled poussin with citrus flavors

Mesclun and tomatoes with Robby's dressing

Figs, honeycomb and cinnamon ice-cream

A day ahead: Marinate poussin; make Robby's dressing; combine cinnamon and ice-cream then refreeze.

Mustard honey glazed vegetables, page 92

IN THE FRENCH MANNER

Red currant-glazed duck

Mustard honey glazed vegetables

Sugared brioche surprises

A day ahead: Make glazes for duck and vegetables; combine prunes and brandy for brioche.

3 hours ahead: Fill brioche.

PAC-RIM FARE

Balsamic and ginger beef

Lemon grass and chili-smoked swordfish

Mixed vegetables

Ice-cream with rhubarb ginger sauce

A day ahead: Marinate both beef and fish, separately; make rhubarb ginger sauce.

1 hour ahead: Prepare vegetables and cumin mixture.

OCEANSIDE FEAST

Tunisian prawns with cilantro potatoes

Sardines in chermoulla with tomato salsa

Seafood brochettes with lime and coconut

Char-grilled vegetables

A day ahead: Marinate prawns and fish for brochettes; make cilantro mixture and chermoulla; toast pistachios.

3 hours ahead: Combine sardines with chermoulla; coat prawns with pistachios; make tomato salsa.

Chicken with caramelized pear, page 34

TAILGATE PICNIC

Sausages with garlic mushrooms

Sweet chili beef ribs

Damper

Tomatoes with feta, olives and cornmeal

Caramel banana pizza

A day ahead: Marinate sweet chili beef ribs; make feta mixture for tomatoes; make caramel sauce for pizza.

1 hour ahead: Make garlic mushrooms.

THE BAJA WAVE

Beef fajitas

Tex-Mex ribs with corn muffins

Nachos sausages

A day ahead: Marinate both the beef and ribs, separately.

3 hours ahead: Wrap tortillas in foil; make salsa to accompany fajitas; prepare vegetables for corn muffins.

BIRTHDAY BARBECUE

Sausages with maple syrup and mustard

Mega beef burgers

Ice-cream or fresh fruit with rocky road sauce

A day ahead: Make beef patties (or make ahead and freeze).

3 hours ahead: Make the rocky road sauce.

LA DOLCE VITA

Garlic and rosemary smoked lamb

Three-mushroom pizza

Arugula and parmesan salad with Italian dressing

A day ahead: Prepare lamb; mix Italian dressing; grate cheeses for pizza.

3 hours ahead: Soak smoking chips in cold water.

Just before serving: Make salad by tossing arugula leaves with Italian dressing; top with shaved parmesan.

Pears with ricotta, date and maple filling, page 100

ENTERTAINING THE NEIGHBORS

Pork steaks with caraway and cabbage

Roasted beets

Pears with ricotta, date and maple filling

A day ahead: Combine date and ricotta mixture for the pears.

FEEDING GOOD FRIENDS

Roasted whole chicken with caramelized lemon

Corn with sage and bacon

Peppered spinach and feta damper

Fresh or barbecued fruit

A day ahead: Prepare corn; soak in combined milk and water.

3 hours ahead: Prepare chicken; press sage and bacon onto corn and tie husks.

AN INDIAN BANQUET

Grilled lamb chops with raita

Chicken tikka with grilled bananas

Cardamom spiced apple pizza

A day ahead: Marinate chicken; make coconut mixture for bananas; prepare apple and cream cheese mixture for pizza.

3 hours ahead: Make raita.

SUMMER IN THE CITY

Apricot chicken

Green salad with honey Dijon dressing

Yogurt with summer berry compote

A day ahead: Make filling for chicken; make honey Dijon salad dressing; prepare summer berry compote.

3 hours ahead: Roll up apricot-filled chicken.

DOWN AT THE BEACH

Lime chicken on lemon grass skewers

Asian-style snapper in banana leaves

Char-grilled fruits

A day ahead: Skewer chicken onto lemon grass and marinate. Make lime and macadamia dressing for chicken skewers.

3 hours ahead: Prepare and wrap snapper in banana leaves; prepare fruit and make syrup.

NEW YEAR'S BRUNCH

Seafood platter

Tossed salad with French dressing

Ice-cream with caramel pistachio sauce

A day ahead: Clean and marinate seafood; make the French salad dressing; make caramel pistachio sauce.

Beef fajitas, page 12

Butterflied hot and sour prawns, page 78

SOME LIKE IT HOT

**Butterflied hot and
sour prawns**

**Ginger pork with mango
and red onion salsa**

**Fresh or grilled fruit with
pineapple coconut sauce**

A day ahead: Prepare and
marinate prawns; marinate
pork; prepare pineapple
coconut sauce.

JAPANESE HIGHLIGHTS

**Ginger tuna with
wasabi drizzle**

**Teriyaki snapper
with soba**

**Steamed rice and grilled
asparagus**

A day ahead: Marinate tuna and
snapper; make wasabi drizzle.

NOT JUST FOR VEGETARIANS

**Baked ricotta with
char-grilled vegetables**

**Mixed seed
beer bread**

**Curly endive and watercress
with Russian dressing**

A day ahead: Prepare and
measure all seeds for bread;
make Russian dressing.

NORTH AFRICAN GRILL

**Quail grilled
North-African style**

**Lemon and artichoke rack
of lamb**

Garlic chili potato kebabs

3 hours ahead: Make seasoning
and cumin dressing for quail;
soak skewers; season quail;
cook potatoes for kebabs.

A SPECIAL OCCASION

**Standing rib roast
provençal**

Orange glazed ham

**Turkey with raisin and
Brazil nut stuffing**

**Potatoes with raclette
cheese and garlic**

**Raspberry pecan bread-
and-butter pudding**

A day ahead: Marinate beef;
make stuffing for turkey;
prepare orange glaze for ham.

3 hours ahead: Season and tie
turkey; wrap potatoes and
garlic in foil.

THAI-TANIC

Thai beef salad

**Snapper filled with
Thai-style vegetables**

Cilantro potatoes

A day ahead: Marinate beef;
mix Thai dressing; prepare
cilantro mixture for potatoes.

WHEN THE BOSS COMES
TO DINNER

**Duck with Madeira and
juniper berries**

**Sugar and rosemary
smoked rump**

**Mesclun salad with
thousand island dressing**

**Strawberry pizza with
mascarpone**

A day ahead: Marinate duck;
make thousand island dressing;
combine mascarpone with sugar
and liqueur for pizza.

AN AMERICAN PICNIC

**BBQ ribs with Boston
baked beans**

Corn on the cob

**Baby romaine lettuce with
Caesar dressing**

Boston brown bread

A day ahead: Soak beans;
prepare and soak corn;
marinate ribs; make Caesar
salad dressing.

Thai beef salad, page 29

Catering for crowds

*Here we have given beverage quantity guidelines when
catering for large crowds.*

750ml bottle beer	= 3 to 4 6oz glasses
750ml bottle Champagne	= 6 x 4oz flutes
750ml bottle wine	= 5 x 5oz glasses
4-liter wine cask	= 26 x 5oz glasses
750ml bottle spirits	= 15 x 1.6oz nips
5-liter cask orange juice	= 20 x 8oz glasses
10 fresh oranges	= 6 x 6oz glasses
12oz can soft drink	= 2 x 6oz glasses
1.25-litre bottle soft drink	= 6 x 6oz glasses
8oz tea	= 80 cups
4oz instant coffee	= 60 cups
1lb ground coffee	= 40 cups
3 liters water	= 25 cups

20lb ice will chill about 24 bottles of wine or about 48 small bottles of beer.

SOMETHING OLD,
SOMETHING NEW

Burgers bellissimo

Jazzy beef sausages

**Ice-cream with lemon and
passion fruit syrup**

A day ahead: Make burger
patties (or can be made earlier
and frozen); make sauce for
sausages; make lemon and
passion fruit syrup.

HEAT MEETS SWEET

**Vodka and Szechuan pepper
glazed chicken**

**Shredded red cabbage with
Russian dressing**

**Date dumplings in
butterscotch sauce**

A day ahead: Make glaze for
chicken and Russian dressing.

1 hour ahead: Prepare blini
mixture to accompany chicken;
make butterscotch sauce.

FLAVORS FROM THE
SPICE ISLANDS

**Blackened fish fillets
with sweet tomato relish**

**Lamb roasts with citrus
tabbouleh**

**Caramelized peaches with
spiced yogurt**

Up to 1 week ahead: Make
sweet tomato relish.

A day ahead: Marinate fish and
lamb; make spicy mixture for
fish; make spiced yogurt.

Lamb roasts with citrus tabbouleh, page 48

Meat cuts suitable for grilling

BEEF

DIRECT HEAT:
rib eye steak
filet mignon
rump steak
rib steak *(with bone-in)*
T-bone steak
boneless sirloin steak *(New York cut)*
sirloin steak with bone in *(porterhouse)*
boneless top
blade steak *(with and without bone)*
tip steak
top round steak

INDIRECT HEAT:
top round roast
blade roast
tip roast
standing rib roast
sirloin roast
rib eye roast
rump roast
eye round roast
tenderloin
ribs

LAMB

DIRECT HEAT:
rib chop
diced lamb *(for kebabs)*
eye of loin
leg chop
loin chop
shoulder chop
tenderloin

INDIRECT HEAT:
boneless loin
boneless shoulder
crown roast
mini roast *(round)*
rack
leg
boneless leg
butterfly leg
four-rib roast
party rack
lamb shank
lamb drumstick

VEAL

DIRECT HEAT:
tenderloin
rump steak
shoulder steak
round steak
rib chop
leg chop
loin chop
eye of loin
eye fillet medallion
cutlet or scaloppine slice

INDIRECT HEAT:
shoulder
tenderloin
leg
loin *(bone-in)*
rump

PORK

DIRECT HEAT:
loin chop
rib chop
loin steak
rump steak
leg steak
loin medallion steak
butterfly chop
diced *(for kebabs)*
spareribs
loin cutlet or scaloppine slice

INDIRECT HEAT:
leg
top loin
rolled shoulder
blade roast
rack
loin
rump mini roast
boneless loin
ribs
tenderloin

ARUGULA, also known as rocket, rugula and rucola; a green salad leaf.

BACON SLICES made from pork side, cured and smoked. **Fat bacon** is the fatty end of a bacon slice, without the lean (eye) meat.

BAKING POWDER a leavening agent consisting mainly of 2 parts cream of tartar to 1 part bicarbonate of soda (baking soda).

BAKING SODA also known as bicarbonate of soda.

BARBECUE SAUCE a spicy, tomato-based sauce used to marinate or baste or as an accompaniment.

BEANS

Black, also known as turtle beans or black kidney beans, are an earthy-flavored dried bean completely different from Chinese black beans (which are salted and fermented soy beans). Often used in Mexican, South and Central American and Caribbean cooking, especially for soups and stews.
Black-eyed also known as black-eyed peas. Available dried or canned.

BREADCRUMBS

1- or 2-day-old bread made into crumbs by grating, blending or processing.

BRIOCHE rich French yeast bread made with butter and eggs. It is available from bakeries or some specialty markets.

horseradish

BULGHUR also known as burghul wheat; hulled steamed wheat kernels that, once dried, are crushed into various sized grains. Used in Middle-Eastern dishes, such as kibbeh and taboulleh.

BUTTER use salted or unsalted ("sweet") butter; a stick of butter equals 1/2 cup.

BUTTERFLIED technique in which chicken, shrimp or cuts of meat are halved horizontally and flattened before cooking.

BUTTERMILK low-fat milk, cultured to give a slightly sour, tangy taste; low-fat yogurt can be substituted.

CHEESE

Bocconcini Small rounds of fresh "baby" mozzarella, a delicate, semi-soft, white cheese are traditionally made in Italy from buffalo milk. Spoils rapidly so must be kept under refrigeration, in brine, for no more than 1 or 2 days.
Feta Greek in origin; a crumbly textured goat or sheep milk cheese with a sharp, salty taste.
Haloumi a firm, cream-colored sheep milk cheese matured in brine; somewhat like a minty, salty feta in flavor, haloumi can be grilled or fried, briefly, without breaking down. Substitute fontina cheese if unavailable.
Mascarpone a fresh, thick, triple-cream cheese with a delicately sweet, slightly sour taste.
Mozzarella a semi-soft cheese with a delicate, fresh taste; has a low melting point and stringy texture when heated.
Parmesan a sharp-tasting, dry, hard cheese, made from skim or part-skim milk and aged for at least a year before being sold. Parmigiano Reggiano, from Italy, aged a

minimum of three years, is one of the best.
Pecorino hard, dry, yellow cheese, which has a sharp pungent taste. Originally from sheep milk, now made with cow milk. If unavailable, use parmesan.
Raclette is the generic name of a semi-hard cheese, which is gold in color with a few small holes and a rough light brown rind. It has a distinct nutty flavor and melts well.
Ricotta a sweet, fairly moist, fresh curd cheese with a low fat content.

CHERMOULLA A spicy marinating paste; consists of parsley, cilantro, garlic, onion, lemon, cumin, paprika, ginger, and oil.

CHILIS available in many types and sizes. Generally, the smaller the chili the hotter it is. Use rubber gloves when seeding and chopping fresh chilis as they can burn your skin. Removing membranes and seeds reduces the heat level.
Flakes crushed dried chilis.
Powder the Asian variety is the hottest, made from ground chilis; it can be used as a substitute for fresh chilis in the proportion of 1/2 teaspoon ground chili powder to 1 medium chopped fresh chili.
Sweet Chili Sauce is a comparatively mild, Thai-type sauce made from red chilis, sugar, garlic and vinegar.

CHOY SUM also known as flowering bok choy or flowering white cabbage.

COCONUT

Flaked dried flaked coconut flesh available in packets.
Milk available in cans and cartons; made from coconut and water.

COUSCOUS a fine, grain-like cereal product, originally from North Africa; made from semolina.

CREAM

Half-and-half (10.5-18% butterfat) a mixture of milk and cream that, like light cream, is sometimes substituted for heavy or whipping cream when lighter, less rich results are desired. Neither half-and-half nor light cream holds its shape when whipped.
Light (contains 18-30% butterfat) also known as coffee or table cream. See half-and-half.
Light Whipping (30-36% butterfat) also known as whipping cream. Its high fat content enables it to hold its shape when whipped.
Heavy whipping (36-40% butterfat) also known as heavy cream.
Sour at least 18% butterfat) a tart, thick commercially cultured product used for dips, toppings and baked cheesecakes. Made by adding an acidifier such as vinegar or lactic acid-producing bacteria to pasteurized cream.

CREME FRAICHE a pourable cultured cream product with a tangy, nutty flavor; sold in plastic containers. To make it at home, heat 1 cup whipping cream to 95°. (Note: do not use ultrapasteurized cream which cannot be cultured.) Pour into clean lidded jar. Add 1 tablespoon buttermilk and shake well. Let stand at room temperature until thickened (12-24 hours). Refrigerate. Makes about 1 cup.

CURRY

Red paste commercial versions consist of chili, onion, garlic, oil, lemon rind, shrimp paste, cumin, paprika, turmeric and pepper. Red paste is hotter than green paste.
Tandoori paste Indian blend of fragrant spices, including turmeric, paprika, chili powder, saffron, cardamom and garam masala.

kaffir lime leaves

lemon grass

kaffir limes

Tikka paste consists of chili, coriander, cumin, lentil flour, garlic, ginger, oil, turmeric, fennel, pepper, cloves, cinnamon and cardamom.

EXTRACTS the byproduct of distillation of plants. Try to buy pure extracts.

FISH SAUCE also called nam pla or nuoc nam; made from pulverized salted fermented fish, most often anchovies. Has a pungent smell and strong taste; use sparingly. There are many kinds, of varying intensity.

FLAX SEEDS The seeds are used for linseed oil and as a flavoring and garnish in Asian cuisine.

FLOUR
All-purpose flour, made from wheat.
Self-rising flour sifted with baking powder in the proportion of 1 cup flour to 2 level teaspoons baking powder.
Rye flour milled from rye.
Whole wheat plain also known as all-purpose whole wheat flour, has no baking powder added.

GARAM MASALA a blend of spices, originating in northern India; based on varying proportions of cardamom, cinnamon, cloves, coriander, fennel and cumin, roasted and ground together. Black pepper and chili can be added for a hotter version.

GINGER
Fresh also known as green or root ginger; the rhizome of a tropical plant. Can be kept in a plastic bag with a paper towel to absorb moisture and refrigerated, or it can be stored, peeled and frozen, in an airtight container.

GREEN GINGER WINE alcoholic sweet wine infused with finely ground ginger.

HERBS we used dried (not ground) herbs. If you need to substitute dried for fresh

herbs, use in the proportion of 1:4 for fresh herbs; eg, 1 teaspoon dried herbs equals 4 teaspoons (1 tablespoon) chopped fresh herbs.

HOISIN SAUCE a thick, sweet and spicy Chinese paste made from salted fermented soy beans, onions and garlic; used as a marinade or baste, or to accent stir-fries and grilled or roasted foods.

HORSERADISH, CREAM STYLE a creamy prepared paste of grated horseradish, vinegar, oil and sugar; less pungent than grated fresh horseradish or horseradish bottled in vinegar.

HORSERADISH, FRESH a plant of the mustard family, with a large white root that has a hot, sharp, pungent flavor. The root is often peeled and grated and used as a condiment.

JAGGERY also known as palm sugar; very fine sugar from the coconut palm. Available from Asian markets. Brown sugar can be used.

JUNIPER BERRIES dried berries of an evergreen tree used as a flavoring.

KAFFIR LIME a medium-sized citrus fruit with wrinkly green skin. The sharp citrus-flavored fruit is commonly used in Thai cooking.

KAFFIR LIME LEAVES aromatic leaves of a small citrus tree bearing a wrinkle-skinned yellow-green fruit originally grown in South Africa and Southeast Asia. Used fresh or dried in many Asian dishes.

KIWI FRUIT also known as Chinese gooseberry.

LEMON GRASS a tall, sharp-edged grass, lemon-smelling and tasting; the white lower part of each stem is pounded or chopped finely and used in Asian cooking or to infuse as a tea.

LIQUEURS
Cointreau citrus-flavored, clear liqueur.
Grand Marnier orange-flavored liqueur based on Cognac-brandy.
Pernod aniseed-flavored liqueur.

MAPLE SYRUP distilled sap of the sugar maple tree. Maple-Flavored Syrup or pancake syrup is made from cane sugar and artificial maple flavoring and is not an adequate substitute for the real thing.

MESCLUN often sold as a salad, and consists of an assortment of edible greens and flowers.

MILK we used full-cream homogenized whole milk, unless otherwise specified.

MIRIN a sweet, low-alcohol rice wine used in Japanese cooking; sometimes referred to simply as rice wine but should not be confused with sake, the Japanese rice wine made for drinking.

MIXED SPICE a blend of ground spices usually consisting of cinnamon, allspice and nutmeg.

MOLASSES a thick, dark brown syrup, the residue after sugar refinement.

MUSHROOMS
Brown light to dark brown mushrooms with full-bodied flavor. Button or cup mushrooms can be substituted for browns.
Button small, cultivated white mushrooms with a delicate, subtle flavor.
Enoki slender 4-inch long body with a tiny head, it is creamy-yellow in color and crisp in texture. Sold in clumps, it has a mild flavor and is good in stir-fries.
Oyster (abalone) grey-white mushroom shaped like a fan.
Shiitake used mainly in Chinese and Japanese cooking.

OILS
Olive mono-unsaturated; made from the pressing of tree-ripened olives. Especially good for everyday cooking and as an ingredient in salad dressings.
Extra virgin and virgin the highest quality olive oils, obtained from the first pressing of the olives.

shiitake mushrooms

brown mushrooms

button mushrooms

enoki mushrooms

oyster mushrooms

113

kiwi fruit

passion fruit

and soy sauce and thickened with starches.

PANCETTA an Italian salt-cured pork roll, usually cut from the belly; used chopped in cooked dishes to add flavor. Bacon can be substituted in most recipes.

PAPRIKA ground dried red bell pepper, available sweet or hot.

PASSION FRUIT also known as granadilla; a small tropical fruit, native to Brazil, with a tough outer skin surrounding sweet-sour pulp and edible black seeds.

red onion

yellow onion

white onion

spring onion

green onion

PASTA SAUCE, BOTTLED a prepared tomato-based sauce (sometimes called ragu or sugo on the label); comes in varying degrees of thickness using different spices to alter the flavor.

PINE NUT also known as pignoli; small, cream-colored kernels obtained from the cones of different varieties of pine trees.

POTATO
Fingerling (German) small and finger-shaped; it has a nutty flavor, and is great baked and used in salads.
New not a variety but an early harvest with a thin, pale skin that's easily rubbed off. Good steamed, and eaten hot or cold in salads.
Pink Fir small with pink to red skin.

POUSSIN a small chicken, no more than 6 weeks old, weighing a maximum 1lb.

Extra Light or Light
describes the mild flavor, not the fat levels.
Peanut pressed from ground peanuts; most commonly used oil in Asian cooking because its high smoke point makes it more suitable for frying.
Sesame, Dark made from roasted, crushed, white sesame seeds; used as a flavoring rather than a cooking medium.
Vegetable any of a number of oils derived from plants rather than animal fats.

ONION
Green also known as scallion or (incorrectly) shallot; an immature onion picked before the bulb has formed, having a long, bright-green edible stalk.
Red also known as Spanish, red Spanish or Bermuda onion; a sweet-flavored, large, purple-red onion that is particularly good eaten raw in salads.
Spring has crisp, narrow green-leafed top and a fairly large sweet white bulb.
Yellow and White are interchangeable. Known as main crop onions they are recognized by their skin color. Their pungent moist flesh (varying in color from white to purple) is very versatile and adds flavor to a vast range of dishes.

ORANGE, BLOOD a medium-sized orange with red or red streaked flesh. It has a sweet flavor.

OYSTER SAUCE Asian in origin, this rich brown sauce is made from oysters and their brine cooked with salt

Roch Cornish hens may be substituted.

PROSCIUTTO salted-cured, air-dried (unsmoked), pressed ham; usually sold in paper-thin slices, ready to eat. Short storage time.

PUMPKIN, NUGGET also called Golden Nugget. Very small, round, orange skin and dark yellow flesh; great baked filled with a variety of seasonings.

RED CURRANT JELLY a preserve made from red currants used as a glaze for desserts and meats or in sauces.

RICE
Basmati a fragrant, long-grained white rice. It should be washed several times to remove grit before cooking.
Short-grain (more correctly called medium-grain) fat, almost round grain with a high starch content; tends to clump together when cooked.

White & wild rice blend pre-packaged blend of white and wild rice. Available from supermarkets and specialty food stores.

RICE WINE a sweet, gold-colored, low-alcohol wine made from fermented rice.

SAKE Japan's favorite rice wine, used in cooking, marinating and as part of dipping sauces. If sake is unavailable, dry sherry, vermouth or brandy can be used as a substitute. When consumed as a drink, it is served warm. To do this, stand the container in hot water for about 20 minutes.

SATAY MARINADE (bottled) a commercially bottled satay sauce. Generally available.

SAUSAGE
Casing Can be purchased from most butchers.
Chorizo Spanish in origin, a highly seasoned, spicy sausage made from ground pork, garlic and red peppers.

SEAFOOD
Boneless fish fillets also known as flake; fish pieces that have been skinned with all bones removed.
Bream also known as yellowfin bream, surf bream and black bream; white flesh with firm fine texture.
Calamari a type of squid.
Lobster sometimes incorrectly called crayfish. The most common varieties are American (Maine) lobster and rock or spiny lobster. Sweet flesh.
Octopus a member of the cephalopod mollusk family. Has a soft oval shaped body and tentacles without any internal shell or "quill". The skin is grey when raw, turning purple/pink when it is cooked.
Prawns also called shrimp.
Salmon fish with red-pink firm flesh; moist delicate flavor; few bones.
Sardine small silvery fish with soft, oily flesh.
Scallops bivalve mollusk with fluted shell valve. We used scallops still having the coral (roe) attached.
Small blue mussels we used the common variety, also known as black mussels.
Snapper small, firm-fleshed, distinctly flavored fish sold whole, good for any kind of cooking method; a number of varieties include red, pink and yellowtail snapper.
Swordfish mild-flavored, firm-fleshed large fish.
Tuna reddish, firm flesh; slightly dry, no bones.

SHALLOTS, also called French shallots, golden shallots or eshalots. Small, elongated, brown-skinned members of the onion family. Grows in tight clusters like garlic.

SEASONED SALT any variety of commercial seasonings blends typically consisting of salt, herbs, spices, and black pepper.

SNOW PEAS also called *mange tout* ("eat all").

SOY SAUCE made from fermented soy beans. Several variations are available in most supermarkets and Asian food stores.
Dark used for color as well as flavor, we used dark soy sauce of Japanese origin.
Light as the name indicates, light in color. We used a light soy sauce of Japanese origin; generally quite salty.

SPINACH
English correct name for spinach; delicate, green leaves on thin stems; high in iron, it's good eaten raw or steamed. Another vegetable often called spinach is correctly known as Swiss chard.
Swiss Chard steam green leafy parts and use as required in recipes.

SPROUTS
Bean also known as bean shoots; tender new growth of assorted beans and seeds germinated for consumption as sprouts. The most readily available are mung bean, soy bean, alfalfa and snow pea sprouts.

STAR ANISE a dried star-shaped pod whose seeds have an astringent aniseed flavor. Used in Asian recipes.

STOCK crumble 1 bouillon cube (or 1 teaspoon stock base) into 1 cup water to make 1 cup of stock. To make your own fresh stock, see recipes on page 118.

SUGAR we used coarse, granulated table sugar, also known as crystal sugar, unless otherwise specified.
Brown an extremely soft, fine granulated sugar retaining molasses for its characteristic deep color and flavor.
Confectioners' sugar or powdered sugar; granulated

flour tortilla

corn tortilla

sugar crushed together with a small amount (about 3%) of corn starch added.
Raw natural brown granulated sugar.
Superfine finely granulated table sugar.

SUMAC a purple-red and astringent spice ground from the berries of shrubs that flourish wild around the Mediterranean (do **NOT** confuse with common name for Poison Ivy); imparts a tart, lemony flavor. Available from Middle Eastern markets. Tamarind concentrate can be substituted.

SWEET PEPPER also known as bell pepper or, simply, pepper. Seeds and pithy membrane should be discarded before use.

SZECHUAN PEPPER (also known as Chinese pepper) small, red-brown aromatic seeds resembling black peppercorns; they have a peppery-lemon flavor.

TAHINI a rich, buttery paste made from crushed sesame seeds; used in making hummus and other Middle-Eastern sauces.

TAMARIND CONCENTRATE (BOTTLED) a convenient liquid form of tamarind, a sweet-tart fruit used as flavoring in Asian cuisine

TAT SOI (rosette pak choy, *tai gu choy*, Chinese flat cabbage) a variety of bok choy, developed to grow close to the ground so it is easily protected from frost.

TOMATO
Paste triple-concentrated tomato puree used to add flavor to soups, stews, sauces and casseroles.

TORTILLA thin, round unleavened bread originating in Mexico; can be made at home or purchased frozen, fresh or vacuum-packed. Two kinds are available, one made from wheat flour and the other from corn (masa).

TURNIP a round, white-fleshed root vegetable. Used in soups and stews.

WASABI an Asian root used to make a fiery horseradish-like sauce traditionally served in small amounts with Japanese raw fish and other dishes.

WATER CHESTNUTS resemble chestnuts in appearance, hence the English name. They are small brown tubers with a crisp, white, nutty-tasting flesh. Their crunchy texture is best experienced fresh, however, canned and frozen water chestnuts are more easily obtained.

WATERCRESS small, crisp, deep-green, rounded leaves having a slightly bitter, peppery flavor. Good in salads, soups and as an ingredient in sandwiches.

WINE the adage is that you should never cook with wine you wouldn't drink; we used good-quality dry white and red wines in our recipes.

YEAST a 1/4oz packet of dried yeast (2 teaspoons) is equal to 1/2oz compressed yeast if you are substituting one type for the other.

YOGURT plain, unflavored yogurt – in addition to being good eaten on its own – can be used as a meat tenderizer, as the basis for various sauces and dips or as an enricher and thickener.

spinach

baby spinach

watercress

arugula

INDEX

Apricot chicken, *38*

Arugula pesto and parmesan Turkish bread, *105*

Asian-style snapper in banana leaves, *72*

Baby beet and arugula salad, Minted lamb with, *50*

Baked fig and date ricotta pizza, *102*

Baked ricotta with char-grilled vegetables, *90*

Balsamic and ginger beef, *22*

Balsamic-flavored octopus, *62*

Basic pizza dough, *106*

BBQ ribs with Boston baked beans, *85*

Beef

    and haloumi kebabs with caper butter, *8*

    and vegetable teppan yaki, *8*

    Balsamic and ginger, *22*

    Braised vinegared, with Chinese greens, *26*

    Burgers bellissimo, *21*

    burgers, Mega, *21*

    fajitas, *13*

    Greek-style, with tzatziki and salad, *18*

    Indian spiced, with dal, *13*

    Nachos sausages, *18*

    New York cut steaks in herbed mushroom sauce, *11*

    Port-smoked, *27*

    rib roast with red pepper crust, *24*

    Rib steaks with bell pepper pesto and sweet potato, *11*

    ribs, Sweet chili, *22*

    salad, Thai, *29*

    sausages, Jazzy, *18*

    sausages with caramelized onions, *17*

    Sausages with garlic mushrooms, *18*

    Sausages with maple syrup and mustard, *18*

    Standing rib roast provençal, *24*

    Stir-fried, with blood orange, *27*

    Sugar and rosemary smoked rump, *29*

    with brandied walnuts and prunes, *20*

    with spiced sea salt crust, *20*

Beet and yogurt dip, *55*

Black bean lamburgers, *56*

Blackened fish fillets with sweet tomato relish, *64*

Blini, *40*

Boston baked beans, BBQ ribs with, *85*

Boston brown bread, *98*

Braised vinegared beef with Chinese greens, *26*

Breads

    Boston brown bread, *98*

    corn muffins, *85*

    Damper, *98*

    Mixed seed beer bread, *98*

    Peppered spinach and feta damper, *99*

    Pumpkin and walnut damper, *98*

Burgers

    Black bean lamburgers, *56*

    Burgers bellissimo, *21*

    Mega beef burgers, *21*

Butter

    caper, *8*

    garlic and chive, *105*

    orange, *42*

    sun-dried tomato, *105*

Butterflied hot and sour prawns, *78*

Buttermilk lamb sausages with onion jam, *57*

Caesar salad dressing, *94*

Caramel banana pizza, *102*

Caramel pistachio sauce, *103*

Caramelized peaches with spiced yogurt, *104*

Cardamom spiced apple pizza, *102*

Carrot and dill rosti, *88*

Char-grilled fruits, *96*

char-grilled vegetables, Baked ricotta with, *90*

Chicken

    Apricot, *38*

    breast, Rosemary-smoked, *34*

    Drumsticks with crunchy satay sauce, *30*

    Lime, on lemon grass skewers, *40*

    Marmalade, with asparagus walnut salad, *41*

    Roasted whole, with caramelized lemon, *36*

    Sticky BBQ, *30*

    Tandoori, with cucumber mint raita, *33*

    Tikka with grilled bananas, *45*

    Vodka and Szechuan pepper glazed, *40*

    wings, Hot hot hot, *39*

    with caramelized pear, *34*

Chili lime snapper, *67*

Chili plum ribs and spicy potato wedges, *85*

Coco-lime fish with papaya-raspberry salsa, *71*

cilantro potatoes, *76*

corn muffins, *85*

Corn with sage and bacon, *90*

cornmeal, Tomatoes with feta, olives and, *93*

couscous, Lamb with pistachio harissa and, *61*

couscous, spiced, Veal shoulder with, *11*

Crab and prawn cakes with salsa, *78*

Crown roast with wild rice filling, *59*

Dal, Indian spiced beef with, *13*

Damper, *98*

Date dumplings in butterscotch sauce, *106*

Desserts

    Baked fig and date ricotta pizza, *102*

    Caramel banana pizza, *102*

    Caramelized peaches with spiced yogurt, *104*

    Cardamom spiced apple pizza, *102*

    Char-grilled fruits, *96*

    Date dumplings in butterscotch sauce, *106*

    Figs, honeycomb and cinnamon ice-cream, *104*

    Maple apples with almonds and mascarpone, *100*

    Pears with ricotta, date and maple filling, *100*

    Raspberry pecan bread-and-butter pudding, *106*

    Strawberry pizza with mascarpone, *102*

    Sugared brioche surprises, *101*

Dips and Accompaniments

    Arugula pesto, *105*

    avocado puree, *68*

    avocado topping, *13*

    Beet and yogurt dip, *55*

    bell pepper pesto, *11*

    cilantro pesto, *69*

    cucumber mint raita, *33*

    Indian chutney, *55*

    Minted pesto, *55*

Olive tapenade, *105*

onion jam, *57*

Raita, *55*

red bell pepper sauce, *68*

Red onion and balsamic jam, *55*

sweet tomato relish, *64*

tzatziki, *18*

watercress and dill pesto, *74*

Drumsticks with crunchy satay sauce, *30*

Duck

    Red currant-glazed, *42*

    with Madeira and juniper berries, *43*

Fajitas, Beef, *13*

Figs, honeycomb and cinnamon ice-cream, *104*

Fish packets with cilantro salsa, *75*

Fish and Seafood

    Asian-style snapper in banana leaves, *72*

    Balsamic-flavored octopus, *62*

    Blackened fish fillets with sweet tomato relish, *64*

    Butterflied hot and sour prawns, *78*

    Chili lime snapper, *67*

    Coco-lime fish with papaya-raspberry salsa, *71*

    Crab and prawn cakes with salsa, *78*

    Fish packets with cilantro salsa, *75*

    Ginger tuna with wasabi drizzle, *72*

    Lemon and mustard calamari, *66*

    Lemon grass and chili-smoked swordfish, *77*

    Lobster tails with avocado and bell pepper, *68*

    Salmon with dill and caper mayonnaise, *78*

    Salmon with watercress and dill pesto, *74*

    Sardines in chermoulla with tomato salsa, *76*

    Seafood brochettes with lime and coconut, *64*

    Seafood platter, *65*

    Smoked trout with potato and apple wedges, *69*

    Snapper stuffed with Thai-style vegetables, *70*

    Sugar and star-anise smoked salmon, *77*

Swordfish with tapenade, *62*
Teriyaki snapper with
 soba, *70*
Tuna steaks with olive and
 feta salsa, *67*
Tuna with cilantro pesto, *69*
Tunisian prawns with cilantro
 potatoes, *76*
French dressing, *94*
fruits, Char-grilled, *96*

Garlic and rosemary smoked
 lamb, *48*
Garlic chili potato kebabs, *88*
Ginger pork with mango and red
 onion salsa, *82*
Ginger tuna with wasabi
 drizzle, *72*
Greek-style beef with tzatziki
 and salad, *18*
grilled bananas, Chicken tikka
 with, *45*
Grilled poussin with citrus
 flavors, *38*

Ham, Orange glazed, *86*
Honey Dijon dressing, *94*
Hot hot hot chicken wings, *39*

Indian chutney, *55*
Indian spiced beef with dal, *13*
Indian spiced lamb with potato
 cakes, *58*
Italian dressing, *94*

Kebabs
 Beef and haloumi, with caper
  butter, *8*
 Garlic chili potato, *88*
 Lamb and artichoke, *52*
 Lime chicken on lemon grass
  skewers, *40*
 Rosemary lamb skewers with
  spiced yogurt, *61*

Lamb
 and artichoke kebabs, *52*
 and bulghur sausages, *57*
 Black bean lamburgers, *56*
 Crown roast with wild rice
  stuffing, *59*
 Garlic and rosemary
  smoked, *48*
 Indian spiced, with potato
  cakes, *58*
 Lemon and artichoke rack
  of, *46*
 Mini roast with horseradish
  cream, *46*
 Mint and lime, with
  salsa, *54*
 Minted butterflied leg
  of, *53*

Minted, with baby beet and
 arugula salad, *50*
Mustard, cutlets with basil
 cream, *52*
Red wine, with garlic
 potatoes, *48*
roasts with citrus
 tabbouleh, *48*
sausages, Buttermilk, with
 onion jam, *57*
skewers, Rosemary, with
 spiced yogurt, *61*
stacks, Tomato and
 mozzarella, *61*
Tandoori, with Indian rice
 stuffing, *58*
with black sesame seed
 dressing, *56*
with garlic and shiitake
 mushrooms, *50*
with pistachio harissa and
 couscous, *61*
Lemon and artichoke rack
 of lamb, *46*
Lemon and mustard
 calamari, *66*
Lemon and passion fruit
 syrup, *103*
Lemon grass and chili-smoked
 swordfish, *77*
Lime and green peppercorn
 quail, *45*
Lime chicken on lemon grass
 skewers, *40*
Lobster tails with avocado and
 bell pepper, *68*

Maple apples with almonds and
 mascarpone, *100*
Marjoram and orange
 turkey, *42*
Marmalade chicken with
 asparagus walnut salad, *41*
Mediterranean pork and
 tapenade roll-ups, *82*
Mega beef burgers, *21*
Mini roast with horseradish
 cream, *46*
Mint and lime lamb with
 salsa, *54*
Minted butterflied leg of
 lamb, *53*
Minted lamb with baby beet and
 arugula salad, *50*
Minted pesto, *55*
Mixed seed beer bread, *98*
Mixed vegetables, *93*
muffins, corn, *85*
mushroom pizza, Three-, *107*
mushrooms, shiitake, Lamb with
 garlic and, *50*
Mustard lamb cutlets with basil
 cream, *52*

Mustard honey glazed
 vegetables, *92*

Nachos sausages, *18*
New York cut steaks in herbed
 mushroom sauce, *11*

Olive and feta salsa, Tuna steaks
 with, *67*
Olive tapenade and mozzarella
 Turkish bread, *105*
onion jam, *57*
onions, caramelized, Beef
 sausages with, *17*
Orange glazed ham, *86*

Pears with ricotta, date and
 maple filling, *100*
pepper and brandy cream
 sauce, Pork chops with, *80*
Peppered spinach and feta
 damper, *99*
Pineapple coconut sauce, *103*
Pizza
 Baked fig and date
  ricotta, *102*
 Caramel banana, *102*
 Cardamom spiced apple, *102*
 Chorizo, *107*
 dough, Basic, *106*
 Roasted vegetable, *107*
 Satay shrimp, *107*
 Strawberry, with
  mascarpone, *102*
 Three-mushroom, *107*
Pork
 BBQ ribs with Boston baked
  beans, *85*
 Chili plum ribs and spicy
  potato wedges, *85*
 chops with pepper and brandy
  cream sauce, *80*
 Ginger, with mango and red
  onion salsa, *82*
 Mediterranean, and tapenade
  roll-ups, *82*
 Orange glazed ham, *86*
 Roast loin of, with crackling
  and applesauce, *83*
 Sausages with toffeed apple
  and sweet-sour leek, *80*
 steaks with caraway
  cabbage, *83*
 Tex-Mex ribs with corn
  muffins, *85*
 Three-pepper, *86*
 with artichoke and spinach
  log, *87*
Port smoked beef, *27*
Portuguese-style seared
 poussin, *36*
potato almond rosti, *56*
potato cakes, *58*

potato wedges, spicy, *85*
potatoes, cilantro, *76*
Potatoes with raclette cheese
 and garlic, *91*
Poussin
 Grilled, with citrus flavors, *38*
 Portuguese-style
  seared, *36*
 with fennel, *36*
 prawns, Butterflied hot
  and sour, *78*
Pumpkin and walnut
 damper, *98*

Quail
 grilled North-African style, *45*
 Lime and green
  peppercorn *45*
 with pancetta and sun-dried
  bell peppers, *44*

Raita, *55*
Raspberry pecan bread-and-
 butter pudding, *106*
Red currant-glazed duck, *42*
Red onion and balsamic jam, *55*
Red wine lamb with garlic
 potatoes, *48*
Rhubarb ginger sauce, *103*
Ribs
 BBQ, with Boston baked
  beans, *85*
 Chili plum, and spicy potato
  wedges, *85*
 Sweet chili beef, *22*
 Tex-Mex, with corn
  muffins, *85*
Roast loin of pork with crackling
 and applesauce, *83*
Roasted vegetable pizza, *107*
Roasted whole chicken with
 caramelized lemon, *36*
Robby's dressing, *94*
Rocky road sauce, *103*
Rosemary lamb skewers with
 spiced yogurt, *61*
Rosemary-smoked chicken
 breast, *34*
rosti, potato almond, *56*
Russian dressing, *94*

Salad
 asparagus walnut, *41*
 baby beet and arugula, *50*
 garlic arugula, *18*
 Thai beef, *29*
 three-bean, *16*
Salmon with dill and caper
 mayonnaise, *78*
Salmon with watercress and dill
 pesto, *74*
Salsas
 cilantro, *75*

mango and red onion, *82*
olive and feta, *67*
papaya-raspberry, *71*
sweet chili cucumber, *78*
tomato, *13*
watermelon and
    mango, *54*
Sardines in chermoulla with
    tomato salsa, *76*
Satay shrimp pizza, *107*
Sauces and Dressings
avocado dressing, *21*
basil cream, *52*
butterscotch sauce, *106*
Caesar salad dressing, *94*
Caramel pistachio
    sauce, *103*
caramel sauce, *102*
cumin dressing, *45*
dill and caper
    mayonnaise, *78*
French dressing, *94*
garlic basil dressing, *52*
Honey Dijon dressing, *94*
Italian dressing, *94*
lemon and mustard
    dressing, *66*
lemon and passion fruit
    syrup, *103*
orange glaze, *86*
pepper and brandy cream
    sauce, *80*
Pineapple coconut
    sauce, *103*
red bell pepper sauce, *68*
Rhubarb ginger
    sauce, *103*
Robby's dressing, *94*
Rocky road sauce, *103*
Russian dressing, *94*
spiced yogurt
    (savory), *61*
spiced yogurt
    (sweet), *104*
Summer berry
    compote, *103*
Thai dressing, *29*
Thousand island
    dressing, *94*
wasabi drizzle, *72*
Sausages
beef, Jazzy, *18*
Beef, with caramelized
    onions, *17*
Buttermilk lamb, with
    onion jam, *57*
Lamb and bulghur, *57*
Nachos, *18*
with garlic mushrooms, *18*
with maple syrup and
    mustard, *18*
with toffeed apple and
    sweet-sour leek, *80*

Seafood brochettes with
    lime and coconut, *64*
Seafood platter, *65*
Smoked trout with potato
    and apple wedges, *69*
snapper with soba,
    Teriyaki, *70*
Snapper stuffed with Thai-
    style vegetables, *70*
spicy potato wedges, *85*
Standing rib roast
    provençal, *24*
Sticky BBQ chicken, *30*
Stir-fried beef with blood
    orange, *27*
Strawberry pizza with
    mascarpone, *102*
Sugar and rosemary smoked
    rump, *29*
Sugar and star-anise smoked
    salmon, *77*
Sugared brioche
    surprises, *101*
Summer berry compote, *103*
Sweet chili beef ribs, *22*
Sweet pizzas, *102*
sweet tomato relish, *64*
Swordfish with
    tapenade, *62*

Tabbouleh, citrus, mini
    roasts with, *48*
Tandoori chicken with
    cucumber mint raita, *33*
Tandoori lamb with Indian
    rice seasoning, *58*
Teriyaki snapper with
    soba, *70*
Tex-Mex ribs with corn
    muffins, *85*
Thai beef salad, *29*
Thousand island
    dressing, *94*
Three-mushroom pizza, *107*
Three-pepper pork, *86*
Tomato and bocconcini lamb
    stacks, *61*
tomato relish, sweet *64*
Tomatoes with feta, olives
    and cornmeal, *93*
Tuna steaks with olive and
    feta salsa, *67*
Tuna with cilantro
    pesto, *69*
Tunisian prawns with
    cilantro potatoes, *76*
Turkey
Marjoram and orange, *42*
with raisin and Brazil nut
    stuffing, *33*
Turkish bread
parmesan, Arugula pesto
    and, *105*

mozzarella, Olive
    tapenade and, *105*
with garlic and chive
    butter, *105*
with sun-dried tomato
    butter, *105*
tzatziki and salad, Greek-
    style beef with, *18*

Veal
rib chops with a three-
    bean salad, *16*
medallions with
    tapenade, *14*
parmigiana, *14*
shoulder with spiced
    couscous, *11*
scaloppine with lemon
    and thyme sauce, *16*
Vegetable cooking chart, *95*
**Vegetables and
Accompaniments**
bananas, grilled, *45*
Boston baked beans, *85*
Carrot and dill rosti, *88*
char-grilled vegetables, *90*
Corn with sage and
    bacon, *90*
dal, Indian spiced beef
    with, *13*
Mixed vegetables, *93*
Mustard honey glazed
    vegetables, *92*
onions, caramelized, *17*
potato almond rosti, *56*
potato cakes, *58*
potato kebabs, Garlic
    chili, *88*
potato wedges, spicy, *85*
potatoes, cilantro, *76*
potatoes, garlic, *48*
Potatoes with raclette
    cheese and garlic, *91*
sweet potato, mashed, *11*
Thai-style vegetables, *70*
Tomatoes with feta, olives
    and cornmeal, *93*
Vodka and Szechuan pepper
    glazed chicken, *40*

MAKE YOUR OWN STOCK

These recipes can be made up to 4 days ahead and stored, covered, in the refrigerator. Be sure to remove any fat from the surface after the cooled stock has been refrigerated overnight. If the stock is to be kept longer, it is best to freeze it in smaller quantities.

Stock is also available in cans or aseptic containers. Bouillon cubes or powder can be used. 1 teaspoon of stock powder or 1 small crumbled bouillon cube mixed with 1 cup water will give a fairly strong stock. Be aware of the salt and fat content of bouillon cubes and powders and prepared stocks.

All stock recipes make about 10 cups.

BEEF STOCK
4lb meaty beef bones
2 medium onions
2 stalks celery, chopped
2 medium carrots, chopped
3 bay leaves
2 teaspoons black peppercorns
5 quarts water
3 quarts water, extra

Place bones and unpeeled chopped onions in baking dish. Bake in hot oven about 1 hour or until bones and onions are well browned. Transfer bones and onions to large pan, add celery, carrots, bay leaves, peppercorns and water, simmer, uncovered, 3 hours. Add extra water, simmer, uncovered, further 1 hour; strain.

CHICKEN STOCK
4lb chicken bones
2 medium onions, chopped
2 stalks celery, chopped
2 medium carrots, chopped
3 bay leaves
2 teaspoons black peppercorns
5 quarts water

Combine all ingredients in large pan, simmer, uncovered, 2 hours; strain.

FISH STOCK
3lb fish bones
3 quarts water
1 medium onion, chopped
2 stalks celery, chopped
2 bay leaves
1 teaspoon black peppercorns

Combine all ingredients in large pan, simmer, uncovered, 20 minutes; strain.

VEGETABLE STOCK
2 large carrots, chopped
2 large parsnips, chopped
4 medium onions, chopped
12 stalks celery, chopped
4 bay leaves
2 teaspoons black peppercorns
6 quarts water

Combine all ingredients in large pan, simmer, uncovered, 1$\frac{1}{2}$ hours; strain.

Can't
boil
an egg?

Sweet Potato Leek and Sage Frittata (*Healthy Eating Vegetarian*, page 28)

...Then
bake it.